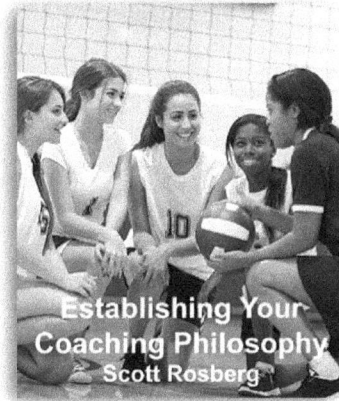

TIME OUT!

How We Can Fix the Problems in Kids' Sports Today

GUIDELINES FOR COACHES, ATHLETES & PARENTS

SCOTT ROSBERG

GREAT RESOURCES
— FOR COACHES —

LIVINGSTON, MONTANA

TIME OUT!
How We Can Fix
the Problems in
Kids' Sports Today
Guidelines for Coaches,
Athletes & Parents

Scott Rosberg

Print ISBN: 978-0-9961320-2-2
eBook ISBN: 978-0-9961320-4-6

Printed in the United States of America

Typesetting & Cover Design: Denis Ouellette
Proofreading: Linda Locke

Great Resources for Coaches
P.O. Box 415
Superior, Montana 59872

www.GreatResourcesForCoaches.com

To Lisa, Maggie, and Morgan—
my most favorite team ever.

Contents

Contents

Preface

When I was a kid growing up in the suburbs of Chicago, every day in the summer, my friends and I would head to the Ben Franklin store, buy enough penny Rain-Blo bubble gum to stuff our pockets, and head out to our grade-school baseball fields to play all day. And I mean, all day! We would get there about 9 in the morning and stay until around 4 in the afternoon. Some days we would go home for lunch, and some days we would pack our lunch. Depending on how many of us were there on any given day, we would play with a pitcher, first baseman, shortstop, third baseman, left-fielder, and center-fielder. If you hit it to right field, you were out, unless you were a lefty. Then, we would all shift positions and left field was out. Nobody taught us how to do all this; we just did it. Well, maybe our older brothers taught us, and it had just been passed down. When we weren't playing, we were watching the Cubs (and occasionally the White Sox) on TV, or buying baseball cards and putting them in shoeboxes or the spokes of our Stingray bikes.

In the fall, we turned to playing touch football in the street. The sidewalk was out of bounds, and you had to deal with the occasional parked car or call "time-out" when a car was coming and "time-in" when the car had passed. We would sometimes don helmets and shoulder pads and play tackle football down at the same school where we had played baseball two months before. I always wore my #51 Dick Butkus Chicago Bears jersey, and my best friend Bob wore his #15 Bart Starr Green Bay Packers jersey. We had the same rivalry with each other at age eight that those two teams have had for over seventy years.

In the winter, depending on the weather and our moods, it was either hockey in the street or basketball in a driveway or back yard. From Bobby Hull and Tony Esposito to Bob Love and Jerry Sloan, our heroes were in every move we made. We would watch games on TV and then try to duplicate on our courts and rinks what we had seen the superstars do. It's how we learned to become the athletes we all became. When spring rolled around, we headed back to the baseball fields and the cycle started over.

Those were some of the best days of my life—just a bunch of kids playing sports without a care in the world. It's where I learned to love sports, and I'm sure it's where I began to develop my understanding of the athletic world in which I have worked for over thirty years. It's probably how you got started playing sports, too. Oh, the names and places are certainly different. Only a handful of you reading this book grew up in the Chicago area in the 1960s. But wherever you grew up, you probably had the same type of fondness for your games and the people who played them as I did. You, too, probably made up rules based on who was there and where you were. You created your own moments that will forever be frozen in your memory, and they all revolved around sports.

I have a 17-year-old boy now, and he absolutely loves sports. However, he hasn't really experienced things like I did growing up, playing with friends out at the ball fields. He tries sometimes, but it's just not ingrained in his friends and him in the same way that it was when we were kids. One of my biggest concerns as he was growing up was that he wouldn't do what so many other kids did and just choose to stay home to watch TV and play video games. Fortunately, my wife and I limited his time on such things, but even doing that, he still spends an inordinate amount of time "watching" life on his phone more than "living" life outside. My hope is that he continues to pursue a life of movement both outside and inside more than a sedentary life in front of a screen.

While the world has changed so much that many kids don't get the freedom to do this, we live in a part of the country where through the years, we have felt safe letting him go out and play with friends. With so many stories today about little kids being abducted, it was hard for us to let him go too far for very long, but he was just fine. Also, the sports world he has grown up in is different than the one I grew up in. At any hour of the day, he can sit and watch games or highlights of sports from all around the world. He sees the highs and the lows of sports on a regular basis. The athletes he looks up to as heroes are plastered all over our TVs, newspapers, magazines and malls, and not always for their wondrous feats of athletic ability, but for their illegal, immoral, or unsportsmanlike feats of stupidity.

A kid's sports world has changed in another way, too. For years I have noticed that when I drive by ball fields like the ones I used to play on, I don't see kids playing out there much unless it's for practice or games. Nowadays, kids don't seem to play any of their sports unless some adult is organizing it and running it. What a shame. I remember hearing a radio talk show host back in Chicago in the late 1980s talking about this very same thing. He had three boys in the 8-to-13-year range, and it was a summer day. He described how his kids were just sitting around the house saying how bored they were. He said, "Why don't you go down to the park and play some baseball?" His son's answer has stuck with me for over thirty years: "Who's going to coach us?"

WHAT? Who's going to coach us?!?! No one! You go down there and you play, and kind of coach yourselves; you live without a coach and just have fun!

That is the sports world we live in today. So many Saturday-morning soccer games, preceded by Monday and Wednesday soccer practices, with soccer camp in the summer, have made many kids believe they can't do any of it without it being organized by someone else. AAU basketball, Little

League baseball, USA wrestling, and any other youth sports activity you can think of, have all added to this dilemma. What do these all have in common? They're run by adults.

As this book will show, there are many problems with youth sports, but without a doubt, the biggest problems of all have come from one source—adults. Adults come in all forms, from coaches to parents to school administrators and teachers, but the bottom line is that most of the problems we face in athletics today stem from the adults. The dilemma is that most of these adults mean well. They just want to find a way for their kids to have a chance to play the sports they love. Unfortunately, it has gotten out of control.

This book is written so that we can look at the problems of kids' sports today and discuss ways and means to fix them together. It is written with both parents and coaches in mind, as well as anyone else who has an interest in the healthy pursuit of sports for our kids. Hopefully, parents of young children will get a chance to read this before they embark upon their child's athletic journey, thus be ready for some of the challenges along the way. Also, those of you who have kids already on their athletic journey will be able to see what we are doing right at present and what we need to do better.

Ultimately, there is one goal for this book—to foster ways for kids to have a positive athletic experience as they grow up. If any of you reading this feel that it has helped you achieve this, please let me know. It will make my day.

Acknowledgments

There are a number of people I would like to thank who were pivotal in the creation of this book. First, I want to thank my parents. While they were not athletic people themselves, they instilled in me so many of the character traits that led to my philosophies on coaching and sport, Their good character and moral fiber and their positive outlook on life modeled for me the way that I wanted to be and the types of things I wanted to instill in my players and coaches.

Thanks to all of the coaches who were inspiring to me, especially those who I have worked with through my years as a coach and athletic director. And yes, I am even grateful for the coaches who inspired me to write because of the problems they created.

Thanks to all my players who I was fortunate enough to coach. You have been the foundation of the greatest elements of my professional career and have made it all worthwhile. While I have enjoyed the strategies, practice planning and running, coaching in games, and all of the other elements that go with the job, nothing comes close to how much I have enjoyed my relationships with you. I loved the time we spent together while I was coaching you, and I have loved the connections I have maintained after our team experiences have been finished. It has been one of the great joys of my life to see "my kids" grow up to become the amazing young men, women, husbands, wives, fathers and mothers that you have become. I can't express to you the joy and pride you have brought to me.

A special thanks to Bruce Brown of Proactive Coaching. Bruce has had such a huge impact on me as a coach, athletic director, friend, husband, and parent. I also know that he has had a profound impact on literally thousands of young people who he has either coached or taught.

My editor, typesetter, cover designer, and self-publishing coach, Denis Ouellette, has been my behind-the-scenes partner. His polishing and expertise are a big part of the final product you see here. That goes for the final proofreader, Linda Locke, too.

Finally, thanks to my wife, Lisa, my daughter, Maggie, and my son, Morgan. They have supported me through jobs that have been extremely gratifying, time-consuming, frustrating, exciting, and filled with extreme highs and lows, all while trying to maintain a family. They have been a huge part of this book because of their involvement in my sports. As Maggie and Morgan grew up, they were involved in their own sports, but I have been a huge part of their experiences, too. I thank them for handling their sport experiences the right way and allowing me to help them in that endeavor. Together with all of my years of coaching, there has been no greater proving ground for the elements of this book than the youth and school sports I have been around in watching them grow up.

Introduction

When I began writing this book many years ago, I had just resigned my position as head basketball coach of a high school boys' team. I had been coaching basketball for seventeen years, eleven of them as a varsity head coach. I had coached at a Catholic high school in the suburbs of Chicago for eleven years, the last six of them as the head coach. I then fulfilled a lifelong dream and moved to the mountains of Montana where I coached for six years in two different towns. I had various degrees of success in both states, taking teams in Illinois to sectional finals and taking my first team in Livingston, Montana to the state tournament. I also coached football in both states, soccer in Illinois, and sixth-grade boys' and girls' basketball in Livingston. I left coaching and then teaching a year later because of some of the frustrations I felt, which I will discuss in this book. However, I couldn't stay away from it for long.

After just a year away from coaching, I volunteered to help out with the girls' basketball team at our school. After one year of doing that, my family and I moved to another state. For one year, I was away from teaching and coaching completely, and I realized how much I missed it. But why? This profession had drained me, burned me out, and frustrated me so much that I felt at the time I would never teach or coach again. Yet here I was, just three years out of being a head coach, missing it so much that I wanted to get back in.

Once I had decided that, though, I didn't just get back into teaching and coaching. Oh no, that would have been the rational, sane way to do it. Instead, I jumped in with both feet into the biggest fire of all—I became an athletic director at a small school in Washington state. Now, all of the frustrations that I had felt as a coach were about to be magnified, because I was now in charge of ALL the sports at both a high school and a middle school. Oh, and on top of that, I also became the high school's varsity girls' basketball head coach. Talk about a glutton for punishment! What was I thinking?

I was thinking that as a coach, I have the ability to affect 10 to 35 young people's lives each year, and as an athletic director, I could affect hundreds of kids' lives each year. More importantly, I would be able to affect coaches who were going to affect hundreds, even thousands, of young people's lives over the years. That idea challenged me, and I decided it was time to do it. After all, I had already started this book, in hopes that I could open some eyes to the problems in youth athletics, and then help to fix some of those problems.

Well, as an AD, I did get to be on the front lines of working to do just that. I left that AD position and took another one in a different state, which I held for four years. I also was coaching basketball at the time. However, after 12 years as an AD, the problems I had to deal with got to be too much. This book will help to explain some of those problems and offer some ways we can work to resolve them.

Ironically, without a doubt, coaching athletics has been one of the most rewarding things I have done in my life. I experienced some of my greatest highs while coaching sports. Some of these highs came in the form of victories, championships, and awards, but the greatest highs were always the joys of developing relationships with the kids—helping them to improve, and teaching them about teamwork, discipline, and the joy of sports—while watching them experience their own highs, knowing that I had in some small way contributed to their good experiences.

Coaching can be one of the most enjoyable and satisfying experiences that one can call their profession. However, coaching can also be extremely frustrating. The profession has changed a lot in the last thirty years, due to many factors. I am writing this book to try to get people to take a look at what has happened that has caused high school and youth athletics to be filled with so many challenges these days.

I hope this book will help other coaches to see what is happening around them. I also hope that parents, players, and fans will start to see the role that they play in the problems, and what we can do together to improve the present state of affairs. Finally, I hope to start to formulate some solutions to the problems that will be discussed. In this way, all the people involved in these situations will be able to take part in fixing a problem before it's too late.

I don't want to paint too grim of a picture—that's not my intent at all. High school and youth athletics are still an important and positive element in any school and community setting. But I do think we need to take a closer look at the current state of athletics and figure out how to make things better. I hope that you, too, will join me in trying to find a better way for our kids to have the positive athletic experience they deserve, with all the benefits it can provide.

Pre-Game Warm-Up

The Landscape of Kids' Sports

1 ❖ What's the Problem?

You may be wondering, "What is the problem with kids' sports? I don't see anything wrong." Let me begin with somebody else's observations on the concept. This comes from a 2014 article by Jay Atkinson, who runs the Methuen Fun Hockey League and the "Skate & Read" program in the Boston area. While it comes from an article about the negative effects that parents have had on kids' sports, the information is important for parents, coaches, and any other adults involved in or who have children involved in sports:

"Single-sport specialization, the privatization of youth leagues, and the ranking and cutting of young children have become widespread. These are not positive trends, and coaches, educators, community leaders, and parents should take heed.

"Three out of four American families with school-aged children have at least one playing an organized sport — a total of about 45 million kids. By age 15, as many as 80 percent of these youngsters have quit, according to the *Open Access Journal of Sports Medicine*. One reason is the gap between the child's desire to have fun and the misguided notion among some adults that their kids' games are a miniature version of grown-up competitions, where the goal is to win. In 20 years of coaching youth and high school sports, I can say unequivocally that adult expectations are the number one problem." (Atkinson)

Telling isn't it? This is just one small glimpse into some of the issues that parents, coaches and a variety of other groups of adults have allowed to seep into the youth sports world.

In this first section, I would like to shed some light on what I see has happened over the years. While my perspective is generally that of a high-school coach, many of these issues also come into play when talking about youth athletics, such as little league, youth soccer, club volleyball, etc. When these issues apply to all young people, elementary through high school, we'll use the catch-all phrase of kids' sports. Anytime I am referring to a particular age group, I will say so.

While I have been a parent for over 17 years, I coached for 18 years without having children of my own. That led me to a lot of my ideas and perceptions on kids' sports from the coaching side of the equation, not the parents' side. In fact, I had a parent use that fact as the basis for an argument with me to explain what she felt was a problem with my coaching. Many parents may have felt that since I didn't have kids, my perspective was skewed.

I can see how a parent would feel that way, and so I didn't just dismiss it as parents being overly sensitive or ignorant. However, I don't think that my not being a parent meant that I couldn't understand some of what people were going through. I was a kid once, too. I remember what types of things my parents and I went through when I was a high-school athlete. I have talked with my parents about those days, trying to gain some insight into what some of my players and their parents go through. I have also talked with coaches who are friends and also parents, to gain their insight. Finally, I have talked with other friends who are parents about their views to try to help me better understand what they go through from their side. All of this has been helpful in me coming to an understanding of the parents' point of view.

And now I am a parent myself. This first happened when I married my wife and assumed the role of step-father to her ten-year-old daughter, who at the time was playing basketball, soccer, and softball. I saw first-hand how easy it is for parents to see the game quite differently than how coaches see it. I felt the urge to yell things out to my new daughter during her games, and quite honestly, there were times when I did. But I tried to yell out only a few times in a game and to only yell praiseworthy things or attitude/behavior things, and to yell to more players than just her.

Suffice it to say that I have a different perspective than most parents out there, but it is a changing perspective, too. It has been ever-changing since I now have a 17-year-old boy. So I have gone through what so many of you as parents have gone through, and my perspective has changed a bit. I started writing this book when my son was little, and I wondered if my philosophy and ideas would change as time went on. For the most part, they haven't.

One other important factor is that I was also a high-school English teacher for eighteen years. As I worked with kids every day as their teacher, and for twelve years as an athletic director, I developed a pretty good handle on what goes on in their lives. In fact, in some ways I may have a better handle than some of their parents, because many of the kids let me into their lives in ways that they would never let their parents in. That does not supersede their relationship with their parents, but it's an adjunct to it. And that points to one of the solutions that I see as important for us to recognize when dealing with problems in kids' sports: parents, teachers and coaches need to work together to understand each other and to meet the kids' needs.

Ultimately, most coaches and parents want the same thing—what's best for the kids. They just have different ideas of what's best for their kids and different ideas on how to get there. However, don't all parents have differences of opinion with parents of their children's friends? Most all parents have thought, at one time or another, "Well, I sure wouldn't let my kid do that!" with regards to something another parent allowed his or her child to do.

We see and hear this time and time again. But how often do the parents then discuss it to see what is really happening there? Not very often, as I see it. This is not much different than the parent/coach relationship, except that the parent is entrusting the child to the coach in an "official" capacity with something the child really wants to do, so the parent seems to feel he or she has more feelings of empowerment to speak up and complain to the coach.

I wish I could very neatly package up an answer to the question, "What is the problem with youth sports today?" and deliver it, so that we could just fix it with some simple salve or glue and be on our way—but it's not that easy. I will outline some of these problems here, adding more detail in the coming chapters, then offer solutions as we move ahead into the future.

Coaches

First, we who are coaches must look in the mirror and view ourselves in a clearer and more realistic way. We must understand the importance of our jobs, place our emphasis on the right things, and see our roles from the proper perspective. While some coaches don't understand the importance of their jobs, others seem to take themselves too seriously. Our jobs and their importance to kids are not replaceable; however, we are replaceable.

Kids

Second, the kids themselves are a part of the problem. Most people will agree that kids have changed in the last fifteen to twenty years. Of course, that is something I heard thirty-five years ago when I started in this field, and I'm sure every generation said it. Do you know why? Because kids ALWAYS change through the years! That's why we have a generation gap. Kids need to be themselves, listen to their own music, play their own games, read their own books, and so on.

Still, what seems to be new and different is how they have changed this time. A loss of respect for others and authority, lack of discipline, and a dwindling work ethic are some of the biggest negatives I see. These changes are greatly affecting not only their present, but also their future.

Let me point out here that I know many people who feel that kids have not changed. What has changed are their parents and society in general. I agree with that, but while the bigger changes have occurred with regards to parents and society, the by-product is a change in kids. Nonetheless, kids and their behaviors have definitely changed over the years.

Parents

Third, as I already alluded to, parents are a big part of the problem with youth sports. Parents must see sports as games that their children like to play and that coaches like to stay involved in by coaching. Parents need to cut the cord from their kids when they start to play a sport. Bruce Brown, a veteran coach and athletic director, and director of Proactive Coaching, tells parents to, "Release your child to the game." However, they still need to love, nurture, and support their kids along the way. This is no different than if the child were in music or the arts, but it is often dealt with much differently for kids in athletics. We will examine the how, why, and what to do about this later on in the chapter on parents.

Administration & Teachers

Fourth, I believe that school administrations and non-athletic teachers are a big problem in school sports. Some administrators and teachers continue to try to stress to kids that athletics are secondary to academics, while many kids try to tell them that they aren't. Administrators and teachers need to understand more clearly that participation in school athletics is what keeps many kids either in school or performing well in school, whether they like it or not. Instead of fighting that and trying to prove to a kid that Renaissance Literature or Geometry are the things that a kid is in school for, administrators need to recognize that anything that makes a kid want to be in school is good. Then we, as teachers and administrators, need to play that for all it's worth, because the dropout rate in many schools around the country isn't getting any better. Administrators and teachers need to give athletics its due, and not treat it like a second-class citizen.

Society & Media

Finally, there are some factors that I will group into the category of societal influences. Elements of this section will be things such as pre-high-school sports, college athletics, professional athletics, money in sports, and media exposure. It is often easy for people to want to blame "society" for all our problems, so I will be careful to avoid doing that. However, to ignore societal influences and the media would not be accurate either, as they have had in many cases a strong influence on the sports our children play. We will explore some of the ways this influence has increased in recent years.

I see youth athletics going in the wrong direction in these five areas more than anywhere else. As I continue to do research and talk with more people, I may find more. Or I may find that some of them are not nearly as bad as they seem. I hope that's the case. Most importantly, I hope that more people can come to an agreement on many of these things. Maybe then we can work towards ways of solving the problems and making athletics what it should be: an enjoyable way for kids to spend their time pursuing something they love, creating a positive experience and great memories, while also finding out more about themselves and the world around them. This is my goal in writing this book. I hope I can be successful on this journey.

One final comment here—this book is not just about what's wrong with kids' sports today. I also see all around me evidence of things that are right about youth sports. Good coaching, parents who are truly supportive, great attitudes from kids, and administrators and teachers who place the proper emphasis on athletics—these all exist in this nation.

Every school has participants who are doing things right. Unfortunately, these people are often the silent majority, or worse, the minority, and they often lose their voice. It's often the vocal minority, the "squeaky wheels," that capture our time and attention. We must rally around the good people we see in our athletic communities, and do all we can to support them. For that to happen on a bigger level, more people need to come to an understanding of what it means to be a good member of an athletic community, from coach to parent to player. When more of the "good guys" are in the forefront, hopefully more of the negative elements will start to fade away. Once that starts happening, real progress can be made. Now let's zero in on each of these areas in more detail.

1st Quarter ~
Coaches

J. Duke Albanese, Maine's former Commissioner of Education and the lead policy adviser for the Great Maine Schools Project, which published *Sports Done Right—A Call to Action on Behalf of Maine's Student-Athletes*, said, "If I had to sum up the crisis in kids' sports, I'd do it in one word—adults." (Relin, 4)

Many people agree with this sentiment. When looking at the adults involved in youth sports, the first group of adults to look at are coaches. There are a few basic problems with regards to coaching that are contributing to the problems in youth sports. As a coach, I am the first to acknowledge that our profession has its share of bad apples in it. It also has other problems than just bad coaches. While I don't believe that we are the biggest problem with youth sports, we are certainly a big problem that needs to be addressed.

Over the last 10 years, I have written multiple books and booklets and spoken at numerous coaching clinics and schools on a variety of topics for coaches. My books and presentations have titles like: *Establishing Your Coaching Philosophy; Playing Time: Guidelines for Coaches, Athletes & Parents; The Sportsmanship Dilemma;* and *The Responsibilities of Coaching*. Each of these and the others are geared toward helping coaches provide a positive athletic experience for kids. It's hard for me to pinpoint the biggest problem with coaches, so what I intend to do here is just go through a list of areas of concern.

2 ❖ Training

The first problem that I see with coaches is that they all too often don't have the proper amount of training in dealing with kids. Often a coach is someone who is in a community where a coaching opening exists. No one else applies for it, so the team, school or league takes the one person who says he or she will do it. While it's nice that this person has volunteered, it's not always a good thing. This person may have no prior experience or no training in working with kids. Yet, because we have a lot of kids who need to be coached, we allow this person to interact with and coach our kids.

Coaches Need Education on How to Coach

This is a situation we often see in the younger grades, such as in Little League Baseball, youth soccer, Pee Wee football, and AAU Basketball. Oftentimes, the coach is merely a father who is reliving his glory days vicariously through his son or daughter. He has never had to deal with kids other than his own. His ideas on how to parent his own children and his limited knowledge of athletics from his own playing days and from watching TV are his only guides to coaching all kids, and this can be a real problem.

A lack of formal training can be a dangerous thing when power is given to inexperienced or unqualified people. We wouldn't send our children to someone who claims to be a counselor or pediatrician for instance, who doesn't have a degree or who has never taken a class on the subject, but who just decided to volunteer his or her time. Would we send our children to schools that have "volunteer teachers" who weren't certified to teach? Of course not! Yet we often allow almost anyone to coach our kids, simply because he or she has volunteered to do so, and we couldn't find anyone else to do it. Why is that?

Well, a couple of reasons present themselves. One is that our kids really want to play this game, and we don't want to let our kids down. After all, it's only a few hours each week. How much harm can it do? Well, there is certainly the obvious concern of the sexual-predator coach to worry about, and I will address the predator coach later. The harm I am referring to when you have coaches who have no training in dealing with kids is not as obvious as the predator coach, and yet is so prevalent that we see it all the time.

Teaching & Modeling Bad Behavior

I am talking about situations where a coach does not instill proper behavior, stop improper behavior, or worse yet, exhibits improper behavior himself or herself. Many behaviors that children in these situations are taught can lead to real problems down the road. Coaches not focusing on teaching teamwork, enjoying the game, being happy for teammates, doing what one is told, and being accountable for one's actions are all hurting the future development of these young people, and not only as athletes.

I have seen kids at young ages allowed to be poor sports or even worse, downright hurtful to other players, and it was not even addressed by their coaches. In fact, I have at times seen that type of behavior applauded by, and even, instilled by their coaches. I have seen those same kids come into the high school sports setting and become the biggest problem that a sports program and the school has to deal with. Had coaches addressed the behavior earlier, some of the later problems might have been avoided. Those types of behaviors then stay with people for most of their lives and not just during athletic competition.

Even worse are the coaches who not only allow such behaviors, but who teach it or who model it themselves. There are coaches who will be living out their own problem lives through the youth or school sports they are coaching. A few years ago, a show began airing on the *Esquire* channel called *Friday Night Tykes*. The show followed a few youth football teams from San Antonio, Texas through practices and games during their season. The children in the games were around 10 years old. The behavior of the coaches was an abomination to football, youth sports, and to sports in general. The language that the coaches used around and to the kids, the methods they used to teach and motivate, and the examples they set for their teams were all so terrible, that it made my blood boil to watch—my blood pressure is rising right now as I type this. One example says it all: one coach had a problem with the upcoming opponent called the Rockets. He led his team through a chant during their pre-practice stretch in which he sang, "F*** the Rockets!" and the players sang it in a unified response. Unbelievable!

Now some people reading this will say, "Well, that's football in Texas for you." First of all, I can't fathom that everywhere in Texas this how football is played. There are many great people in Texas who would never stand for such behavior, even in their football. However, if people were to make that an excuse for how football is taught, coached, and played in Texas, and it was true that it is usually played that way, then Texas football needs to take a serious look in the mirror and figure out what it needs to do to get it right.

Also, don't tell me that Texas is the only place in the nation where that kind of bad behavior in football is happening, and don't tell me football is the only sport where coaches behave that way. Bad coaches and bad coaching behavior are prevalent everywhere in this country, in every sport and at every level. It is imperative that parents and kids step up and address such behavior when they see or hear it. They need to address the coach and address the leadership of the leagues in which these people are coaching.

Another reason we will let just anyone coach our kids is that we sometimes have an attitude about it that seems to say, "At least someone will do it, so why not let them? I mean, as long as I don't have to do it, then it's okay." Again, we must think of the consequences of that type of thinking. We don't think that way when it comes to selecting a daycare for our children. Why then do we allow it in sports?

Ironically, for some parents, sports are a form of daycare, giving them some time away from their kids, yet they don't investigate the coach and the program in the same way they would a sitter or a daycare provider.

Required Coaching Classes & Training

I am not saying that without the training many of the volunteer coaches or paid coaches don't ever do a good job. In fact, it is amazing how many of them actually do a great job without any real training. What I am saying is that if a child's involvement in athletics is so important to him or her and to parents (and I believe it is), then there should be required coaching classes in order to coach. Many states around the nation are now requiring that school coaches take coaching classes and/or coaching effectiveness programs in order to coach, and they often have to pass a test when they complete the program. The National Federation of High Schools has a Fundamentals of Coaching course that many states around the country make their high-school coaches take in order to coach.

I think this type of training is a good start to address this problem. How about making this mandatory in all states? Moreover, how about making this mandatory for coaches of all ages and all levels, not just for high school coaches? There are youth-sport coaches (AAU basketball, volleyball and wrestling, Grid Kids football, Little League baseball, youth soccer, etc.) who need this more than anyone. For most kids, this is their first taste of organized sports. The impressions they have of how organized sports are supposed to work get formed at this level first. The coaches at these levels are working with some of the youngest, most impressionable kids out there, yet they have no training in how to do it properly.

Monitor & Evaluate the Systems, Programs & People

Even scarier, there is no check and balance system on many of these coaches. As a high school athletic director for twelve years, I worked with high-school and middle-school coaches in my programs to help them learn various methods and philosophies for good coaching. We interviewed prospective candidates and looked for qualities of character and discipline. Once we hired people to coach, I tried to coach them, too. I worked with them and brought in others to work with them on proper methods for dealing with kids, parents, standards, guidelines, situations, and more. I did this with all of our coaches, not just the new ones. And, I also had some leverage with our coaches. If they didn't handle themselves properly, it could show up in a poor evaluation, they could be reprimanded or even fired. There was accountability for their actions.

There is very little or none of this in most of the youth-sports world—anyone with a pulse can coach a team. There is no one working with them to be better coaches, no one guiding them, and no one monitoring them. Now I know some youth-sports directors are going to read that and say, "That's not true. When we see coaches acting out of line, we reprimand them." A few questions come to light: How far out of line does one have to get? Ask any parent with a kid involved in youth sports if they have seen any coaches act in ways that they and many others deem out of line, and you will hear a resounding, "Yes!" Still, these coaches continue to coach without ever being reprimanded or even confronted. Also, where are the directors who are monitoring these coaches? Are they at all of the games? Is there an evaluation process that the coaches are being put through?

I coached the high-school girls' basketball team in Washington during the summers in an AAU setting for my first three years there. I also saw AAU games for boys and girls of all ages held in our gym each year that I was there. The leagues ranged in age from first grade through high school. During the fall and winter, we had approximately six to eight teams practicing and competing, and this did not include our high-school and middle-school aged kids. There were AAU practices in our gyms on a nightly basis after our school teams practiced. Then there were games on Saturdays. This was happening all up and down the valley in which I lived. I know it was also happening all around the state, but the league/division of which our teams were a part focused on our valley. There were roughly fifteen communities ranging in size from 800 to 65,000 all involved in this one league. How could a director or even a handful of directors "see" all the coaches who were coaching in that league and know if they were out of line? The answer, of course, is they can't.

However, they may say that each community has its directors who run their programs. Good point. Let's look at the "directors" in our community. One was a man who was about 50 years old. He was a great guy and a great supporter of the youth in our community. In fact, he was the person who started the AAU program there about twenty years ago. However, he had no training in coaching. He had no training in training coaches. He had no training in education. He was like so many others who do this. He was a dad who wanted his kid to have a chance to play and develop as he grew up.

The other director of the AAU program in that community was a woman who also had kids in the program. She was, and still is, the middle-school secretary. She played basketball in high school. She, too, had no formal training in coaching or in dealing with coaches. Again, she had kids who were at the age where she wanted them to play and develop. I heard her complain at times about some of the coaches in the league that she was "in charge of," but there was little to no action taken to address issues. And who could blame either of these two people? They had no formal training in how to coach or direct other coaches, and the coaches themselves had not been trained in any fashion on how to coach. The system was set up for problems to occur.

I know of veteran coaches at the high-school and middle-school levels who feel that they have been coaching long enough, so that they shouldn't have to do any training in coaching. While I understand that experience is a great teacher, what would be wrong with getting some additional training in the general aspects of coaching? What are these veteran coaches afraid of? I would fall into the category of a veteran coach, and my thinking is, if it helps strengthen my abilities as a coach and it strengthens the caliber of coaching for all, then let's do it.

How about youth sports such as Little League baseball? The horror stories we have heard from Little League, and more recently youth soccer and hockey, are appalling and quite often they involve the coaches. Why not require these coaches to complete the type of coaching effectiveness program I spoke of earlier?

Let's train all coaches properly, so they can train our kids properly. Even having a coaches' workshop or seminar for a day or weekend prior to the season would be a start. In this workshop, issues such as discipline, treatment of players, dealing with parents, how to teach skills, dealing with other coaches, and so on could be addressed. Then we would at least have some uniformity among the coaches in these leagues.

3 ❖ Money

One final reason why we may be so lax in our allowing anyone to coach is a lack of money. I would imagine that there are many people out there who think that we coaches make a darn good buck. They see that the new head coach of the New York Jets or the University of Kansas is making $5,000,000, and they assume that all coaches make good money. Don't be fooled. That kind of money is only being made at the pro and college levels, and only at the very top programs. From there it drops off quite quickly. I have heard that in Texas, high-school football coaches get paid a very good regular full-time salary just to coach. I have also heard that those coaches are treated a lot like college coaches in that, if they have a bad record for one season, they could possibly be fired. That's a huge problem in and of itself, if that is the case, and that needs to be addressed, too. That may only be the case in Texas and a few other pockets around the nation, but it is not the norm. Let me clue you in on how it has been for my colleagues and me over the last few years.

From 1982 to 1993, I taught and coached at a Catholic high school in the suburbs of Chicago. In my last year there, for being the boys' varsity head basketball coach, I made approximately $3,000. I moved to Montana and taught and coached at a public school from 1993 to 1999. In my last year there, I made just under $3,500. In 2006, in my last year as a head basketball coach at a small public school in Washington, my salary was $4,385. In 2015, in my fifth year as the boys' head basketball coach at a high school in Montana, I made $4,875. That means that after being on the job for over twenty-five years, I was making $4,875, and that is an average salary in our conference. So please, don't tell me that coaches make good money.

Now I know that some people will say, "So? It's not a full-time job." Hah! High school basketball season in my state officially begins on the Friday prior to Thanksgiving week. (That's a couple of weeks later than many states, by the way.) We have 2-to-3-hour practices that take up to an hour to prepare, to set up the gym, and to put everything away. Once the games begin, our average home game had me there from 3:30 until 9:30 pm. On away games, our average bus trip was two hours. So, for away games add 2 to 4 hours, plus an hour stop to eat on the way home. I coached in tournaments where we were gone for two and three days at a time. We played eighteen games from the first week of December until the final week of February, and then came post-season playoffs. If we were fortunate, we went to the state tournament in the first week of March.

When the season ended, we did all our inventory, evaluations, and awards. Then we began to prepare for the off-season. We started kids in the weight room in the springtime. The first week that school was out for the summer, we had an evening shooting camp for high-school kids and a weeklong camp in the mornings for kids in grades 5 and 6, and in the afternoons for grades 7 and 8. The next week, we had a week-long camp for our high-school kids. (This, by the way, was the only thing I ever made any extra money on, over and above my coaching salary. In my last year coaching our summer camps, I made $400 for running two weeks of camps.)

We played in summer tournaments on weekends in June. Of course, we needed to practice to prepare for those. Depending upon which schools I have been at, summer-league games were usually two nights on a weeknight in June and into July for both JV and Varsity. We went to about four tournaments that ran Fridays, Saturdays, and Sundays. We also hosted one of these. We also opened the weight room once a day, three days a week, throughout the summer. In October we would start our conditioning program and our open gyms. This ran up to the first week of the season. So as you can see, this may not be a full-time job—it just looks, feels, smells, and tastes like a full-time job—sometimes even more than a full-time job!

This problem is not just one that high-school coaches face; it is also not only about paying coaches a good salary. There just isn't enough money in our schools and city recreation departments to be able to pay coaches what they're worth or to pay for coaches' education classes and workshops. We have heard that time and time again. Well, quite frankly, I'm sick of it. There is no more important job in America today than that of a teacher and coach. We need to start paying our teachers and coaches better than we pay greeters at Wal-Mart. When we start offering salaries for teaching and coaching that are competitive with other business-type salaries, then we will draw a better workforce to the profession. When that happens, we will all start to win the battle again.

For too long, academia has been the poor stepchild to the business world when it comes to salaries and finances. At the same time, athletics has been even lower than academia in this respect. It's about time we changed that. Our government leaders need to recognize the impact that youth sports and interscholastic sports have on our young people who will some day be the adults running this country. Many of these leaders played sports when they were younger, and they often tout the value and impact it had on their lives. In 2004, Brian Kilmeade compiled the stories of over seventy people in America who became famous or hugely successful in a book called *The Games Do Count*. All of these people, from presidents to CEOs, to television personalities, talk about the impact that playing sports had on the success they eventually experienced. These stories are an important reminder that we need to find ways to fund athletics and activities programs so that quality people today can help develop quality people tomorrow.

At the beginning of this section on coaches, I mentioned the *Sports Done Right* document that the University of Maine created as part of its Great Maine Schools Project. One of their core missions was improving the quality of coaching. J. Duke Albanese said, "The most powerful mentors kids have are coaches. Coaches don't even realize the extent of their influence." *Sports Done Right* recommended that coaches not be compensated with bonuses based on win-loss records. Rather, compensation should be based on their level of training (Relin, 6). That concept is right in line with the teaching world. The more continuing education credits a teacher has, the further up the salary scale s/he goes.

This is a good idea for coaches as well. Rather than basing pay on which sport someone coaches or on longevity, how about compensating coaches more for more coaches' education hours acquired? As for coaches in non-school youth sports, we need to find a way to compensate them. At the very least, we need to find funding to pay for their training and for coaches' education programs. While it is not only about money, money helps to incentivize people into it that might not otherwise do it. Once you are paying people or paying for their training, you can demand a little bit more from them. They are no longer just volunteering their time, so you can hold them to a higher standard. That way, we can start to make some progress in creating better coaching in youth sports.

4 ❖ Perspective

Win at All Costs

The next problem I see with many coaches is their perspective. They are misguided on what is important and what is not. This comes in many forms. First, there is the win-at-all-costs mentality that is so prevalent with too many coaches today. I myself am competitive and hate to lose. I am all for trying my hardest to win every time I step onto the field or court. When I go out and play one-on-one or five-on-five basketball with my teams or with my friends, I want to beat that opponent of mine, and I get upset if we don't win. However, that does not mean I will allow the goal of winning to supplant all aspects of athletic competition. Too many coaches focus only on winning.

Dan Campbell, two-time state champion track coach at Edward Little High School in Maine, says he sees too many of his peers pressing to win at all costs. "One coach can destroy a kid for a lifetime. I've seen it over and over." (Relin)

There are numerous examples out there of coaches who have lost their perspective. Every one of you reading this could cite a story of someone you know or have heard about who had coaches whose perspective was so warped that they went overboard due to this win-at-all-costs mentality. What usually happens on these types of coaches' teams is that the high-scoring players will play most of the time, while lesser players will play very little. The kids displaying less talent start to enjoy it less and lose the sense of fun that has been associated with sports and the team experience. These kids often decide to quit.

Anytime a coach starts to have such a negative impact on kids (especially at younger ages) that the kids are thinking about giving it up, it is time to be concerned. It is time for the parents to meet with the coach.

Now, please understand, I don't believe in parents jumping in and talking to the coach in any situation that comes up with their child's sport. I think the child should speak to the coach and learn to work out the situation on their own. Too many parents want to save their child from every dilemma that they go through. However, those kinds of moments and conversations can help a child learn valuable lessons. But in situations where young children are thinking about quitting because it is no longer fun, it's a good time for the parents to step in.

If the child's discussion with the coach and then the parents' subsequent discussion do not yield any results, then it might be time to speak to the athletic director or the director of the league. Parents need to be able to talk to a superior who can then talk to the coaches about their behavior to try to help them improve at their ability to work with kids. So many young athletes are at crucial ages in the development of their sports life. We cannot have coaches who quell their kids' enthusiasm for sports. On the contrary, they should be doing everything possible to develop and nurture their enthusiasm.

As I think back to when I was nine, I am struck by how much I loved Little League baseball and how important my coach, Mr. Kelly, was to my enjoyment of it. I would have loved baseball no matter what, but I loved Little League because I had such a positive experience, largely due to Mr. Kelly. Had I had some jerk coaching me who didn't care about us as kids and only cared about winning, I would not have had such a great experience.

So, come on, coaches! Remember you are dealing with kids. These are impressionable young people who want to play, and learn, and develop, and grow, and make friends, and most of all, have fun. Yes, they want to win. So did I, and so did Mr. Kelly. But winning is just one part of the overall experience. Kids aren't focused on it as the be-all and end-all of playing on this team and neither should you.

Deserving Victory

There are many lessons to learn in athletic competition other than winning. One of the first things I like to instill in players on my teams is the idea of "deserving victory." We need to teach kids that they must do things like work hard, play together, be a good teammate, be disciplined, and so forth before they ever should expect to win. In this way, student-athletes learn that, in order to have success, one must put in the time and effort necessary to achieve success. If you don't deserve to win, then winning is not nearly the same.

Dealing with Losing

Another important skill that coaches can help to instill in their players is how to deal with losing. We will all lose at certain things, and how we deal with loss says a lot about us. We can learn how to react to loss, learn from it, and become better able to avoid it the next time, if we are taught how to deal with it properly.

But too many coaches don't help players understand that losing is part of the nature of competition. I am not advocating that we teach kids to accept losing. I want my players to hate to lose, but I also want them to be able to be dignified and classy after a loss. There is no place for a player or a team to not shake hands with an opponent after a clean, fair, hard-fought game. There is also no place for a coach to berate and belittle players after such a game, just because they lost. We as coaches need to serve as the role models in this situation. Good sportsmanship is one of the most important things a coach can instill in his players.

Just Have Fun & It's Only a Game

On the other side of the win-at-all-costs issue is the coach who "just wants the kids to have fun." I understand the importance of them having fun, and I tell people all the time that that's why kids play sports in the first place; however, eventually as players get older, they get more competitive. It's no longer fun just going out, goofing around, and going through the motions. Winning becomes part of what is fun.

Just walk into a winning locker room after a game, and then walk into the losing locker room. You tell me who is having fun and who is not. And if the losing team is having too much fun, there's a problem there. While I want my players to keep it all in perspective, I don't just tell them, "Hey, it's only a game." I would never do that to someone who has put so much effort, sweat, emotion, and sometimes blood into something.

Oftentimes the people who say it's only a game have never played in such a game. There have been times when I've watched kids play a sport that I had little experience with. Mainly these were children of friends of mine. I too have said to them after a loss that it's only a game, but I realize now it was a game that I knew very little about, and that I really didn't know what I was talking about. It was unfair of me to tell them that it's only a game.

Now, when I talk to someone who has just lost a game, I say very little. I usually try to say, "Nice game," or "You gave great effort," (if they did), and "I really enjoyed watching you play." I let the child dictate if he or she wants to talk or not. If the child wants to talk, then I try to talk about what was done well by the team and then the individual athletes, and to keep in mind that they played hard or well or together.

Yet, I believe strongly that we shouldn't diminish their competitiveness and determination. We need to help them continue to channel that drive in a positive direction and realize that winning and losing are part of the entire process. While I will admit that too many of us focus on who won, let's remember why they do have a scoreboard. We cannot let them become satisfied with losing, but they should never be satisfied with winning either. Also, these ideas are aimed at dealing with athletes in the grade ranges of junior high school and older.

Younger children should be focused more on enjoyment and development and not so much on winning. At the same time, they need to be taught about how to deal with winning and losing. It is at this younger level where we are seeing the greatest increase in problems with regards to winning and losing. So much of the problem revolves around the fans in the stands and the coaches on the sidelines, but the kids are part of the problem, too. I will certainly talk about the fans' and the kids' roles later in the book. At this level, though, coaches need to always remind themselves why they are doing what they are doing. Focusing on winning games at levels younger than middle school is just the wrong way to coach. The entire experience at this level should be set up to allow kids to have a fun, positive experience, and to help them develop as players.

Long Term Athletic Development

In his book, *Changing the Game*, former soccer player, coach and league director John O'Sullivan explains so many important elements that coaches and parents need to keep in mind when looking at the focus of youth sports. O'Sullivan discusses the concept of Long Term Athletic Development (LTAD) and the stages that kids go through as they develop as athletes. The concept of LTAD comes from the Canadian Sport For Life (CS4L) organization. According to O'-Sullivan (pp. 80–81), the CS4L came up with a list of major issues affecting Canadian sports, such as:

- Young athletes not learning proper movement and fundamentals
- Inexperienced coaches at crucial developmental stages
- Overemphasis on competition and the formation of bad habits
- Under-emphasis on training prevents the breaking of bad habits
- No streamlined developmental system—pulling kids in all directions
- Conflicting environments—no fun, poor skills, poor performance, and ultimately, kids giving up on athletics

- Parents not educated in developmental principles
- Sport specialization occurring at too young of an age

Each of the elements on this list is important to recognize as being problematic as we try to help kids grow, develop, and enjoy their sport experiences. The CS4L recognized these problems and came up with their Seven Stages of LTAD. The stages (pp. 83–84) are as follows:

- Active Start (ages 0–6)
- FUNdamentals (girls 6-8; boys 6–9)
- Learn to Train (girls 8-11; boys 9–12)
- Train to Train (girls 11-15; boys 12–16)
- Train to Compete (girls 15-21; boys 16–23)
- Train to Win (girls 18+; boys 19+)
- Active for Life (any age)

O'Sullivan (p. 90) goes on to point out that "in Canada, Australia, and Great Britain, national sport federation have adopted the LTAD principles into their sport-specific curriculums and are changing the way sports are run at the highest levels."

Unfortunately, the United States has not followed suit, largely due to a lack of any official governing body for youth athletics. "In the United States we have no central sports authority that governs all sports, and thus we depend upon a loose conglomeration of federations, associations, and governing bodies that vary from sport to sport, even state to state." O'Sullivan points out that while the rest of the world is catching up to us in terms of international sport success in which we have historically been highly successful (i.e., basketball, golf), some of the organizations realize that we need to change our mindsets when it comes to instilling the LTAD concepts into youth sports.

Thankfully, a few governing bodies in American sports are beginning to encourage the LTAD model. Soccer, swimming, and hockey, for instance, have recognized that the current system is broken. Unfortunately, the national federations have very little say over the actions of all the various entities that sponsor their sports. It seems this is starting to change. O'Sullivan says (p. 91) that it will change even more as parents are educated about the importance of LTAD.

The CS4L has pointed out (pp. 92–93) ten key factors of LTAD that it would be wise for coaches, parents and athletes to learn so as to be prepared to better understand how to maximize the athletic experience for all kids. These ten factors are:

- Ten-Year Rule
- FUNdamentals
- Specialization
- Developmental Age
- Trainability
- Physical, Mental, Cognitive, and Emotional Development
- Periodization
- Competition Planning
- System Alignment and Integration
- Continuous Improvement

When coaches are not focused on the Long Term Athletic Development of their athletes, they are doing their kids a disservice. For those who are all about winning games, they are missing an essential element of why kids play. This is true at any age and level, but it is critical at the youngest ages up into the mid-teens.

The first age where the term "compete" comes into play in LTAD is 15 for girls and 16 for boys. Prior to that, it should be all about fun, developing, and training. Unfortunately, too many youth coaches are focused on winning games, and they are hurting the sports they coach because of it. They play the "best" kids all the time, set up plays only for those kids, and demand execution at a level that is impossible for many of the kids at that age to accomplish, then berate kids for losing, or for not performing at the expected level of play.

It is amazing every time I hear stories of coaches who have gone over the edge in terms of their desire to win games at the youth sport level. One of the most disturbing stories from a few years back involved a coach offering $25.00 to one of his players to throw a baseball at the head of a nine-year-old handicapped teammate in practice, so the injured boy wouldn't be able to play in an upcoming game. The league rules mandated that all healthy children on a team need to play three innings, and this coach wanted to win so badly that he didn't want the child, who was autistic, to play because it would jeopardize their chances of winning the game. Obviously, this man completely lost all sense of perspective for the games kids play, and he should not have been allowed to coach kids in any way ever again.

Player Development & Improvement

A second area of perspective that coaches often fail to focus on is player improvement. This is the focus of Stages 2, 3, and 4 in the LTAD model. I believe that one of our biggest jobs as coaches is to try to instill in players the idea that improving as much as possible should be one of their ultimate goals, and that success can be measured by improvement as much as by the scoreboard. Let's face it—not everyone has the same talent level. If your only barometer of success is winning, your ideas are skewed.

Back when we were in our primes, if I were to play Michael Jordan in games of one-on-one, I would lose every time. But if after the fifteenth game, I was losing 15–8, instead of 15–0, then I would have gained some level of success! It's the same with our kids.

One of my favorite personal success stories was with a team I coached a few years ago in Darby, MT. It was a small school of about 200 kids. They hadn't won a game the year before, and in the two years before that, they had won three or four games combined. I knew I was not inheriting a team of all-star talent. However, what I did inherit was a team of players with a hunger to improve. They first needed to learn discipline, then a hard-work ethic, and finally the importance of team play. They grew and developed and improved as much as any team I have ever coached. We won our first game of the year and their confidence level rose. While we ended up winning only two games all year, their improvement was phenomenal. We were competitive in almost every game we played. Instead of losing by 25 and 35 points like the years before, we were losing by from 2 to 10 points.

Again, we don't need to instill in players that it's okay to lose. It was hard for me to deal with losing games that much since I wasn't used to it, but I was extremely proud of those players and how they improved. I moved to another town the next year, but my assistant coach took over the team and continued to instill those same fundamentals and principles. They continued to improve on their record to a point where they became a .500 team that year and then continued to get better in the following years under his positive leadership. As a coach, it's satisfying to be a part of something like that, and it's important to make sure our kids feel that as well.

Discipline

Where else do coaches go wrong with regards to the proper perspective of athletics? Coaches need to recognize the importance of instilling and then maintaining discipline. Discipline is a tough one. Some people hear the word and think that it means punishment. Discipline is a great word, a positive word. It is not punishment. Bruce Brown, in *Teaching Character Through Sport*, defines discipline as "focused attention and effort." The great, but often controversial, college-basketball coach, Bobby Knight says that discipline is "knowing what to do, knowing when to do it, doing it to the best of your abilities, and doing it that way every single time." (Brown, 1001 *Motivational Messages & Quotes*, p. 103)

Both of those definitions get to the heart of what discipline truly is. It only becomes punishment when one does not do those things properly. When you stray off the path of discipline, someone else has to put you back on that path. That is where a coach, a teacher, a parent, or some other leader comes in. Just because one coach yells at his players a lot and another one doesn't is not an indication that the first coach has good discipline and the second one doesn't. Good coaches set up standards and rules and then apply them properly.

Notice that I didn't say they stick to those rules as absolute. This is where some coaches run into trouble. They set up rules but then stick to them in such a way as to create more problems than was ever intended by the rule in the first place. I have done this on more than one occasion.

For example, in my early years as a head coach, I had a very strict dress-code rule. I did that at the Catholic school in Illinois because the school had the same dress code that I used for our team. However, when I started coaching at the public school in Montana, I tried to use the same dress code. It didn't work nearly as well, and I ended up having to punish kids for dress-code infractions that really weren't all that bad. I learned to be more flexible. Through the years, I have learned that not all situations are the same. You need to make your rules specific enough to pinpoint certain things, general enough to cover a variety of things, and flexible enough to treat each situation in its own unique way.

The key here, though, is to first have the standards and rules and then to follow up on them. Set up rules that are fair for the situation and for the kids involved. Then, do not let kids get away with thinking that your rules don't mean anything. They need to know that there are consequences for their actions. However, the consequences need to be commensurate with the infraction. For instance, suspending kids for a full game the first time they are five minutes late for a practice is going overboard.

Also, kids need to know that you are in charge, not a piece of paper. I believe the key here is not the rule itself so much as it is your handling of the rule. And for Pete's sake, if you say, "No," make sure you mean, "No!" Too many kids don't hear "no" enough anymore, and when they do, it too often means, "No, not now, but maybe if you keep whining about it." You can still change your mind later or adjust your rules, but you need to make sure that you are firm and consistent with your standards.

So discipline is a key ingredient to the success of any young athlete. If you want to help kids have a positive athletic experience, make sure you instill discipline. Hold them accountable. When you say practice starts at 3:30, if they show up at 3:32, make sure that you address it in some way. "Dave, practice starts at 3:30. You got here at 3:32. That is unacceptable on this team. You are letting your team-mates down by being selfish with your time. This is your one warning. The next time you are late, you will sit out the first quarter." (Or half or whatever you decide.) Then, by all means, if he is late again, make sure you follow through on what you said you would do, or you will lose the respect and discipline of your entire team.

However, before you do any of this, make sure you have given the team a Policy Sheet that outlines your standards and guidelines, so the kids know what to expect. This is critical to your success in establishing your discipline. You don't have to make it cover every single possible situation that could exist—that's impossible. Write it so that it is general enough to cover all situations, but specific enough that you can deal with those situations when they come up. Talk to other coaches and ask to see what their policy sheet is like. Then create your own that you are comfortable with and that you can follow and enforce. (See Appendix A for a Sample Policy Sheet)

I don't mean to paint a picture that coaches must all be stern taskmasters to kids. On the contrary, most of the best coaches out there are compassionate people, but they show it by establishing standards and rules and by being firm, fair, and consistent with them, while at the same time, being flexible and human with their kids. The best coaches set up the parameters that the team must follow, and then work to provide the kids the best opportunities for success within those parameters.

Finally, maybe the most important thing about discipline is that once you do instill it and then maintain it fairly, make sure your kids know you care about them. I try to make sure that my players know after I have had to punish them in some way that I'm still okay with them, and that it was the behavior that made me upset, not them. Kids have fragile egos and psyches, and we must keep that in mind in order to maintain a positive learning atmosphere.

The days of the boot-camp-sergeant, in-your-face, ranting and raving coaches are gone (or at least they should be). While some would say losing that type of coach is a big problem with sports, I disagree. You don't have to be a lunatic to get kids to do what needs to be done. We don't need to coddle them and change their diapers, but we need to let them know that when all is said and done, we care about them. The great NBA coach Hubie Brown would say in his clinic talks that after you have gotten on your players, "You gotta' hug 'em, baby." I've always liked that idea.

One word about standards and rules. For the first half of my career, I was a huge rules guy. I had many different rules set up to try to cover everything that could occur. Invariably each year, something would happen for which I did not have a specific rule, so I had to figure out how to handle that situation and then add a new rule for the next year. After many years of this, I realized that I couldn't have a rule for everything that might occur. I realized, though, that the Standards and Expectations sections of my Policy Sheet were covering everything that was happening.

Standards should be written in such a way that they show people how to live within the framework of the organization, as opposed to rules that show how NOT to do things. Standards are more general than rules, so they allow leaders the latitude to lead. People will rise up to meet standards. When they don't, coaches can address the violations of the standards and determine appropriate disciplinary action. I adopted a policy of focusing more on the team's standards than on the rules. Ironically, that shift has led to much better discipline within our teams. It also has fostered in me the ability to handle the discipline better because I have been able to deal with each situation in a specific fashion, under the guideline of the standard rather than a strict interpretation of the rule.

Excuses & Finger-Pointing

Another important area where coaches need to keep the proper perspective is teaching kids not to make excuses for their failures and not to point a blaming finger at others. Kids often make excuses for their failures. This often comes from their parents making excuses for them as they grew up. As they get older, they can't accept the fact that maybe they have a flaw or that they made a mistake, so they make an excuse or they blame someone else. Coaches need to step in immediately when kids do either of these and make sure the kids are held accountable. That doesn't mean we ridicule them and make them tell everyone else they were wrong. It means we don't let them get away with saying that it was the referee's fault they missed shots or their teammate's fault they dropped passes—even if it's partly true. Coaches need to stop that behavior from happening and let the players and the team know that it will not be tolerated.

We as coaches also need to rise above the temptation. Coaches should not point fingers at others, especially referees. I know how difficult it is to not do this at times, but we must. I will talk with officials, occasionally in a raised voice, and try to get them to see my side, but I will not blame them for our losses. There are too many factors during a game that contribute to the final outcome to blame it all on the referee. The problem is that, if I succumb to blaming, can I excuse my players from doing it too? I don't let my players talk back to officials or make faces or yell at them. That is not part of their job as players. As the coach, I am allowed to communicate with the referee as part of the game, so I do, but I need to make sure I do it in the right way.

Remind players that we are all human, and we all make mistakes. Players need to know that it's okay for them to make mistakes, and it is okay for their teammates to make mistakes, too, as long those mistakes are made at full effort and attention. In fact, mistakes made at full effort and attention need to be dignified because you want your kids to play without fear. If players are concerned about making mistakes, they will not put forth the maximum effort needed. So when you have players who give it their all and still make mistakes, make sure you let them know that it's okay to make those mistakes. Then teach them what they need to know to not let it happen again.

While we want our players to eliminate mistakes, we must recognize that they will make them. We can continue to stress that they need to keep working to reduce their mistakes, yet at the same time, we must show them we understand that everyone makes mistakes. I think coaches are often afraid to admit that they made a mistake because it may show a weakness in them. That's foolish! We are humans just like our players, and they need to be reminded of that.

I have often said to my players after a game that no one made more mistakes than I did out there. I want them to know that I am part of this, and I too have a responsibility to try to do my best, and that I will not always do things perfectly. I think my players have liked that because they knew that I wasn't going to always blame them for our failures.

I have heard coaches who say that players win games and coaches lose them. While I like the sentiment of taking pressure off of kids with that kind of statement, I don't agree with it. I believe it should be that players and coaches win and lose games together.

Ego

This leads to another area that coaches need to work on: their egos. Coaches need to keep themselves in perspective. I have seen too many coaches who take themselves way too seriously. I have always felt that we need to understand the importance of our job, and we must take it seriously, but we must not take ourselves so seriously. We are just one part of the entire equation involved in our sport.

Let's face it—when it is all said and done, probably 80–90% of the time, the team with the better players is going to win. Coaches certainly have an impact on those odds, but it's the ability of the players that more often than not determines the outcomes of games and seasons. Yes, a great coach can make a huge positive difference in any team, no matter the talent level of the players. But the teams with more talent will consistently win games throughout the course of any season in any sport. That is one of the many reasons coaches want their players to work in the off-season—to improve their talent to give them the best possible chance at success.

Too many coaches see themselves as being the show, being the all-important element that makes it all work. While we are certainly a major component of any program, we are still just that: a component. We must push aside our own egos, and keep ourselves in perspective. I hear many coaches talk about themselves when they discuss their games and their teams. They often say things like, "I beat him last year, so he's going to try to get me this year," referring to other coaches. Notice the pronouns "I" and "me" in the previous sentence. We need to get rid of the singular pronouns like "I," "me," and "my" and replace them with plural pronouns, like "we," "us," and "our." Remember, coaches don't play against other coaches; they coach teams that are playing against other teams.

Coaches who think and speak in singular pronouns have the wrong focus. A major focus of youth sports should be to develop young people. Notice I didn't say young athletes. Certainly, athletic development of these people should be a focus. But it shouldn't be the only focus. We must realize that most of these young men and women will never be college athletes, let alone professional athletes. However, they will grow up and be members of society who will need to know how to compete, work with others, handle criticism, help others succeed, and so on. These are all qualities and skills that athletics can teach people. Let's make sure that as coaches we don't forget what our priorities should be.

Ego also hurts coaches when they think that they don't have to learn more or do more work because they already have it all figured out. This is not too shocking with veteran coaches, but it is a problem. Veteran coaches can learn a lot more about the game than they already know, and they can learn from a variety of sources. I have always listened to my assistant coaches a lot because they see the game differently than I do. Also, it doesn't matter how much experience they have or don't have; anyone can help you improve as a coach. However, too often older coaches shut themselves off to younger coaches because the older coach feels, "I've forgotten more about this game than you'll ever know." What a joke! We all come to the table with different knowledge bases, and we can all learn from each other.

The more amazing situation to me, though, is when the coach who won't listen to others is young and inexperienced, but his ego is so large, he won't listen to others who can teach him more. I have seen this for years in high school coaching. It most often happens with young kids fresh out of college who have begun coaching and who were players themselves, especially the ones who were good players. It also happens with youth coaches who have never coached before. This is their first chance to coach, and they're going to show people what they know.

I have been amazed at how some rec-center or youth coaches have also done this. One personal example for me came from years past. I have put on coaching clinics for rec-league/youth coaches in the communities in which I have lived in order to help them learn a bit more about how to coach. I did one for the first time in the town in which I was living about 20 years ago. We had fourteen coaches out of a total of sixteen in the league show up. That was a good number of coaches interested in improving themselves and learning more about how to coach.

The next year I did two clinics a few days apart for the same organization, so we could make sure all the coaches had a chance to attend. Two coaches attended one clinic and three attended the other. The majority of coaches in the league had never coached or had only coached for two or three years. These were free, three-hour-long clinics and still, only two and three coaches showed up! Are you kidding me? Why were the coaches in this league coaching? Did they really want to help the kids? Then why wouldn't they help themselves? It boggled my mind then, and it still does to this day.

Coaches, we need to keep things in perspective by looking in the mirror, checking our egos, and getting over ourselves. We need to be our best so that we can help our kids become their best and have the best possible athletic experience they can have.

5 ❖ Coaching Styles

The next area to discuss with respect to coaches is their style. There are as many coaching styles as there are coaches. However, as Rainer Martens shows in his coaching book, *Successful Coaching*, most coaches fall into one of three general styles: Command, Submissive, and Cooperative. Let's look at these three styles.

Command-Style Coach

When most of us think of a coach, this is probably the first thing that comes to mind. We think of the General, the Dictator, the "My way or the highway" coach. Many of you are right now thinking of someone in particular. This is what that classic stereotype of a coach has always been. Why? Because for so many years, that's how most coaches coached. The coach had absolute authority, and whatever the coach said, that's what you did. In order to get there, many coaches scared or intimidated players into doing what the coach wanted them to do.

It worked because times were different. Parents parented that way more. Classrooms were run that way, too. Kids expected that more in all aspects of life where there was an adult leader. Now, times have changed. It's much harder to get kids to buy into that method for a variety of reasons: breakdown of family structures, relaxed moral standards, child-centered parenting, cable and satellite TV, the Internet, and a variety of other elements.

Now when a coach is an "authoritarian," the coach's authority often gets challenged by players and parents. In some ways, it's a good thing. Some coaches went way overboard and were way out of hand in their dictatorial behavior, especially at the youth levels. However, there are many aspects of this style of coaching that are still important to instill today, maybe more so than ever.

Things such as discipline, accountability for actions, work ethic, respect for authority, and doing what you are told by a superior are all things that come from this style of coaching, and I believe we need them. However, intimidating, grabbing, belittling, hurting, and demeaning players have no place in athletics. We can instill discipline, work ethic and team play without resorting to these behaviors. I believe that elements of the command style are beneficial, but they must be tempered with other elements that we will look at in a minute.

Submissive-Style Coach

The submissive-style is basically there to facilitate children's free time or the coach who does not want to work on instilling discipline in the team and the players. Through the years, we have mainly seen this coach in the community youth sports or in the younger grade sports in schools, although this too has been changing. He or she acts like a playground monitor or intramural director. There is not much real coaching going on, or the coaching that is going on is all about playing and not about working to improve individually or as a team. This coach is just providing time, place, equipment, and a bit of organization to the young people's play time.

This coach is a non-functioning leader. This coach often feels that the kids should just be here to "have fun." While this is a nice thought, this coach is missing the point. The child wants to have fun certainly, and fun should be a part of the game. But part of that fun is learning the game, being on a team, competing hard, and striving to win the game. It's not just rolling out the balls and letting them play around. The kids can do that on their own; they don't need a coach for that type of situation. They need a coach so they can learn the game, learn how to compete, learn how to be a teammate, and learn the proper behavior in an athletic arena. So, if you're going to be a coach, then coach!

I think sometimes these coaches are this way because they don't know enough about the game. Maybe they are doing the job because their child asked them to do it, and they have no background or understanding of the game. Then, they don't want the kids or parents to know that, so instead of working to find out about the game and how to coach it, they just say that it's about kids having fun, so they don't need to do as many things as other teams. These coaches are doing their players a disservice. These coaches need to learn the game and then teach it. There are books, videos, DVD's, and other coaches where a coach new to a sport can learn more. They need to understand the importance of teaching the sport to these young athletes.

More importantly, these coaches need to teach discipline, work ethic, team play, sportsmanship, and respect. You don't need to know a ton about a specific sport to teach these things, and these are some of the most important things we can teach young athletes. I have long maintained that a good coach could probably coach most any sport if he or she were given a couple of good books and videos on the sport and a mentor or two to get ideas from. Similarly, a bad coach probably won't be able to coach any sport no matter how much he or she knows about that sport. The reason is that all the knowledge in the world won't matter if you can't get your players to show up for practice, behave properly, listen to you, listen to each other, work together, or play hard. So coaches need to keep in mind that they do need to teach the sport-specific skills, but they better teach the proper behaviors as well. The submissive coach does neither of these, and should therefore change his or her ways or let someone else do it.

Cooperative-Style Coach

The cooperative coach has also been called the democratic coach. However, I don't like that term as much unless we clarify it. To me "democratic" automatically brings up thoughts of voting on things. And while I believe that occasionally it is good to have teams vote on things, it should not be the normal way of doing things. So I prefer to think of this coach as the "cooperative" coach.

What ideas does the word "cooperative" conjure up? Well, someone who works with others is one thing it brings to mind. That's a good trait for a coach to have. Cooperative indicates someone who listens to input from others. That's good, too. Also, someone who is cooperative is willing to do what it takes for others to succeed. That's exactly what a coach needs to be. Unfortunately, in this day and age, when someone is cooperative, they are often thought to be weak. That's a shame. There is nothing weak about working with others to bring out the best in the group. That's called good leadership. Still, the cooperative coach has to ensure that he or she is still the one in control.

This is where I believe we need to bring in elements of the command-style coach and blend them with the cooperative-style coach. A coach needs to establish the standards, rules, and guidelines of his or her team. The coach needs to infuse those standards into the program and enforce the rules fairly and consistently. The coach needs to instill a strong work ethic, a focus on teamwork, and be cognizant of always teaching good sportsmanship, while at the same time recognizing each individual on the team as an individual. The coach's control must be strong but understanding. The coach must establish the guidelines, but then work with players within those guidelines. The coach must tell players what to do and how to behave, but he or she must listen to players' concerns and questions. Finally, the coach must be doing all this for the good of the entire team. These are just some of the ways that a coach can combine the elements of cooperative coach with command coach in order to be a good coach.

Earlier I mentioned Rainer Martens book, *Successful Coaching*. It is a book I highly recommend any coach pick up. In the section on Coaching Styles, he gives some examples of some specific problematic styles of communication that some coaches have within the scope of the general styles described above. He lists many different styles, such as pretentious, negative, judgmental, and screamer. It is worth it to take a look at his list, and then try to figure out if you fall into one of these categories. If you do find yourself falling into any of the categories, it is critical that you work on your skills to improve your ability to communicate with your players. (We will talk about communication in more detail in the next chapter.)

Coaches need to constantly evaluate their own style and work to have balance in that style. Watching tapes of oneself and listening to comments from other people about one's coaching style are ways to perform such an evaluation. Coaches should look at themselves as honestly as possible to find out what type of coach they are and then figure out what they need to do to improve in terms of their style.

6 ❖ Communication

Good communication is essential to good coaching, no matter what age the athletes are. Athletes need clear-cut directions to understand what they are supposed to do. They get easily confused, and a poor communicator for a coach will lose them. A coach does not have to have a Master's Degree in Communication, but s/he does need to know some basics on communicating with people, especially young people. If not, then poor communication will result, and in many ways poor communication can lead to poor coaching. This needs to be done at all levels. Athletes of all ages need very clear instruction on how to behave, perform, and work. If we start communicating clearly with them very early in their lives, then they will be that much better by the time they are in high school.

Unfortunately, many youth sports coaches have had little or no training with regards to communication skills. Coaches who are also classroom teachers have at least had some education in their teacher preparation on communication skills. However, most youth sport coaches are not teachers. Many have had no schooling past high school, and their high school years were a long time ago.

As I think of the AAU coaches that were coaching in the community I lived in a few years ago, we had two farmers, a secretary, a maintenance man, a factory worker, a college student, an ex-teacher/coach, and a part-time janitor/part time laborer for the county. Other than the college student and the ex-teacher/coach, these people had little or no advanced training in communication skills. This is not meant to be critical of those people. Many of them did a wonderful job coaching. It is merely to illustrate why it is so important for youth sport coaches to receive some training on teaching and coaching in general, not just about the specific sport they are going to coach.

So much of good coaching is linked to good communicating, so it is essential for coaches to have some understanding of communication skills. As I said earlier, some kind of coaches' education for our youth coaches should be mandatory to help them get the proper training in communication skills necessary to help them coach well. We make our teachers go through four years' of college, including a teacher preparation program because we know the importance of this. We need to offer something to our coaches, as well, to help them do the best they can.

Be a Teacher

So how does a coach communicate properly? A coach needs to be a teacher. I don't mean that all coaches need to be certified teachers, but that they all need to recognize that one of their primary jobs is to teach young people how to play the game they are involved in. That may seem obvious to most people, but it is how one teaches that is important. While not all coaches need a formal education in teaching, it is helpful to know some basics about teaching. After all, one of the reasons teachers have to go through college is to learn the hows of teaching, not just the subject matter. If that weren't important, then there would be no degrees in education. People would just get their degree in a field, never take a teaching class, and then go out and teach. So let's look at some of the hows of teaching for coaches.

Organization

Practice Plans

First of all, coaches need to be extremely organized. The first way to be organized is to have a written practice plan. Just like classroom teachers use lesson plans to keep the lesson organized and flowing, coaches use practice plans as a guide for the day's practice. You should spend a good amount of time developing the plan. Make sure to either cover all aspects of the sport every day, or focus on certain aspects one day and other aspects the next.

Whichever way you choose to do it, make sure that there is teaching going on for all of the elements that athletes need to be prepared for. Good practice plans include comments and key terminology that you want to make sure the kids hear. Also, drills should be planned down to the minute. Drills should rarely go more than ten to fifteen minutes. Keeping the pace moving along will help the practice flow better, and it will help keep your players alert and focused. There are many different styles of written practice plans. The key is to have one that is effective for you and your sport.

Teaching the Game

Another area of paramount importance when it comes to coaches being organized is in being prepared to teach the game. That's because once you start teaching a skill or concept, all eyes and ears are on you. You are being judged by your players on everything you say and do. If you are not prepared in all aspects of what you want to say, how you want to say it, and how you want it to sound, you are inviting trouble.

Now keep in mind that for a two-hour practice, you will be teaching and re-teaching many skills and concepts. You need to be prepared for all points that you want to make, all questions that may be asked of you, and all scenarios that could then follow once you actually start working on those skills and concepts. And this happens every time you step into practice. So do yourself a huge favor—come to practice extremely well-prepared.

Keep It Simple

One thing to consider as you are planning your practice situations is that you should assume nothing about your players' knowledge, understanding, and execution of the game. Don't think for a second that these kids already know something, or that they already know how to perform a certain skill even if that skill was taught to them last season. Slippage occurs. People forget things, especially kids.

As a varsity basketball coach at four different schools in three different states, I still had to start the first practices of every year with the most basic elements of the game: how to dribble, pass, shoot, get into a defensive stance, and so on. And I coached some very smart kids and good basketball players at all four schools. It's just that over the course of the year, they forgot some of the basics. It didn't take them long to pick things back up, but we had to start from the beginning. So when your fifth graders aren't understanding the proper way to do something, teach it to them!

Break It Down

Next, break it down. One extremely effective way to teach is in a Whole-Part-Whole method. This means you show the whole thing you are trying to do first, then break it into parts to work on, then work on the whole. The Part section is where you take specific aspects of the whole and work only on those. You may work on one part today, another part tomorrow, and still another part the next day.

The reason for doing it this way is to give them the big picture (Whole), so they understand what you are trying to accomplish. Then have them work at simpler aspects of the big picture (Part) to achieve success. Then bring it all together (Whole) to see how the big picture has now improved. That's why they call it the Whole-Part-Whole method.

Again, while you plan practice, being well organized will really help out in being prepared to teach things by using this method. Think through everything you want to teach, how you want to teach it, and what you want your players to pick up from your teaching. Plan how you will show them the Whole, how you will break it down into the Parts, what you will work on in the Parts, and then how and when you will go back to the Whole.

Correct and Re-Teach

Another important aspect of teaching properly is to correct and re-teach. Don't let players continue to do the wrong thing. This just reinforces bad habits, not only for the players making the mistakes, but also for their teammates. Don't be afraid to correct your players. You will not damage their egos and psyches if you just make sure you do it in such a way that you don't hurt, belittle, or demean them. Yelling at them, "You idiot!! Why are you doing that?!" would fall into the category of hurting, belittling, or demeaning. Just stop the incorrect behavior, re-teach it, and have them work at it again. This is coaching, and it makes up a good portion of the time that we spend coaching.

I am still amazed at the number of coaches I see who do not want to do this. They are either afraid of correcting the player, or they don't want to take the time to do it, or maybe they aren't really sure how to correct it and re-teach it. My thought is that the coach better lose his or her fear of correcting, take the time, or figure out how to correct the problem because otherwise, that kid and the team will all suffer. And by all means, when a player finally gets it right, no matter how small a thing it is, praise the successful action in front of everyone, again not in an embarrassing, belittling way, but sincerely.

Repetition & Emphasis

Another important aspect with regards to teaching is repetition. You must constantly repeat the skills and drills that you are working on. To work on something once or twice and believe that it is mastered is setting your players and your team up for failure. Why in basketball do we have them shoot 10 to 20 to 50 free throws everyday? They know how to shoot them. It's because we want them so confident at the free throw line that every time they go there, they have a good chance at success. Then why don't we treat other aspects of the game that way? Why do we feel that if we do something else a couple of times it should be habit? All aspects of the games we are teaching need to be repeated numerous times to generate the success we are seeking.

Also, once you continue to repeat a certain skill or concept, you are placing emphasis on it. When your players feel you are cmphasizing something, they will work at it harder, for they will feel its importance. The key here though is working at it to show its emphasis. I have spent many years telling players the importance of something, hoping they would see that I was emphasizing it. However, if we didn't work on it a lot, they never felt that it was as important as other aspects that we did work on a lot. Inevitably, those would be areas of weakness until we started emphasizing them by working on them.

Unfortunately, there are only so many minutes in a day's practice, and sometimes you have to sacrifice emphasizing some areas that you feel are important for others that you feel are more important. Again, your organization is critical here, so you can prioritize what you want emphasized most.

Precision

Finally, there is the concept of precision. It is very important that coaches say and show precisely what needs to be done. Speaking in vague and ambiguous terms will only lead to confusion. Also, a coach must not only say precisely what s/he wants done, but the coach must also show it. The coach needs to get out on the floor and walk the players through the situations or have someone else do so. The coach may need to physically demonstrate, move, move players, point to spots, etc. While doing this, s/he needs to be explaining precisely what needs to be done. Once again, being organized will make this process go a lot smoother.

Good Communication

While the aspects of teaching discussed above are important "whats," we must once again emphasize communication skills as elements that are critical to teaching/coaching success. It is so important to good coaching that we communicate clearly. Yet, all too often I see coaches far too concerned with what they're saying and not nearly concerned enough with how they're saying it. Who cares what offense you are running if the players don't understand how to run it?

Enunciate & Speak Up

So what are some elements of communicating so as to be understood? First, enunciate clearly. Make sure that what you are saying is coherent. This is not always easy in a gymnasium, ice rink, pool, or outdoor field setting. There are often a lot of distractions. Hence, it is even more important to speak clearly. Also, speak slowly enough to be understood, but not so slowly that you lose their attention.

You need to speak loud enough to be heard by all, but not so loud that you are the distraction. Again, this is important in many practice settings. You may have to contend with other practices going on, cheerleaders, planes overhead, weather conditions, or traffic. Players need to hear you over these. Remember, they don't always ask questions, even when they didn't hear what you said. So make sure they do hear you.

Repeat It

Along with enunciating and speaking up, repetition in communication is critical. We spoke of using repetition in your drills, but you should also repeat what you say numerous times. This leads to a very important point: Use key terminology to help your communication. Pick out terms and phrases that you are constantly repeating to your players all year long. This will help them quickly pick up what you are saying and what you want them to do. Also, it will help with the transfer from drill to drill and from drills to games. Let me give an example to illustrate.

One basketball coach I worked with named Jim introduced me to a great term that he got coaching at another school. The term was "China Wall." It was a term used to explain where the help side defenders should be on the court. If they were "on the Wall," they were fine. If not, they were "in China," and that's not where we want them to be. (We play in the USA.) So in explaining our drills we would show them where the China Wall was and explain where to be in relation to it. Then as we ran our drills, we would say things like, "Get on the

Wall," and then eventually, we would just yell, "China Wall, Jimmy!" Then we would transfer this into games and yell the same thing out onto the floor. I imagine people in the stands were wondering why we were talking history or geography to our players, but our players all knew exactly what we were talking about. This is a good example of the importance of using key terms and how simple it is to do.

Demonstrate It

Another very important point of communicating clearly is to show and demonstrate everything. Now this is where some people think, "Oh no, I can't do that. I don't have the ability to…" block a kill in volleyball, or throw a discus, or whatever skill in any sport you are trying to teach. Two responses come to mind for that. First of all, it's ok if you can't perform an action. Just make sure you know how to teach the performance of that action, and have someone who can perform the action do it for you. Show everyone how to do it while the player is performing the action. In other words, walk him or her through it to demonstrate. But don't just point to places and say, "Do this" or "Do that." They need to see exactly how to do what you are asking them to do.

The second response I have is, "If you can't perform it, is it something too advanced for your kids to perform?" I'm not saying that coaches do this a lot. However, I know that in my years of coaching, I have asked kids to try to do some things that it turned out they just weren't capable of doing. I was just too stubborn at the time to figure out that I was asking them to do things they physically could not do. Notice though, I am only referring to physical things. They can all behave in certain ways or think in certain ways that you are asking them to. Those things should never be compromised.

On the flipside to the question, "If you can't do it, is it too advanced?" is this idea for the coach who was a superb player at the sport he is coaching: "Just because you could do it, don't assume they can." The head baseball coach at the first school I ever taught and coached at was, from all I was told by many people, a great baseball player when he was young. He had been a catcher when he played. One day in practice when he was coaching, he was working with the catchers on their throws down to second base. He was getting quite frustrated with the young catchers who were constantly missing their target. Finally, he jumped in, grabbed a mitt, and angrily said, "Look. It's real simple. You catch the ball, you hop up, and you fire it to the bag," as he caught a pitched ball and threw a perfect strike to the shortstop's glove right on the bag.

Now, while that was obviously very impressive, what did it teach the players? Well, it probably reinforced the idea that their coach had been a very good catcher. It probably also created a whole lot more pressure and stress on them because now they probably figured they had to live up to that kind of standard. There is nothing wrong with setting the bar high for your kids. Just make sure that you don't make it so high that they don't believe they can get over it.

Questions

Communication is a two-way street, so what about kids asking questions? I have always maintained that a coach should encourage questions from players. However, there are some guidelines to this. I have not always agreed with the concept that there is no such thing as a stupid question. I taught high school English for eighteen years, and I sure heard my share of stupid questions. Most of these were due to the student not paying attention in the first place or being so preoccupied with asking a question, that s/he never heard the answer was already given.

This occurs in coaching as well. This often happens as the players are standing around listening to the coach explain something, like a new drill. Many times they are not focused on what is being said, or they are waiting for a chance to point out a problem. Sometimes they have a question that comes up while they are listening to the explanation, and they don't hear the coach cover the answer to the question.

Therefore, the first thing I tell my players about asking a question is to pay attention while I am explaining something. If they don't understand, they can ask their question when the explanation is finished. If there are no questions or once all questions are answered, we expect them to be able to go full speed through the drill or play. If they can't do that, we tell them to step out of the drill and watch until they get it. However, they shouldn't be sitting out for too long, or we will confront them on it.

How and Why?

The second guideline on questions is to differentiate between "How" and "Why" questions. I never had a problem with a player asking "How" something is to be done. They are trying to perfect the skill or strategy we are implementing. However, "Why" questions can be a problem depending upon the situation. To ask "Why" we are doing something might not be the worst thing. If a player is trying to better learn the game and the reasoning behind why we play the way we do and why we would go to a certain strategy, that is fine, as long as it is done at the right time, and it is done respectfully and within the scope of what our team standards are.

However, sometimes "Why" questions can be problematic when they are done out on the floor or on the field. In practice, we try to limit the number of questions so as not to disrupt the flow of practice too much. I also don't want us to be getting into philosophical discussions on the floor or field during practice. That can sometimes lead to situations where a coach may feel a player is challenging her or him in front of the others. This is a situation that should be avoided. If a player has questions on why we do things the way we do, it is fine for him or her to come in at some other time when we can sit down and discuss the whys. That way, we can diffuse a potential problem, if there is one, in the privacy of a one-on-one office setting, instead of on the court in front of an entire team and who knows who else? The key here, though, is to listen to the intent in the question and then deal with it accordingly.

Listen

The final element of good communication is to listen. It is very important for a coach to listen to a variety of sources and in a variety of ways. Coaches need to listen to players, parents, assistant coaches, administrators, friends, friends of players, etc. As you can see, a coach needs to listen to everybody around him or her. Anyone may be the next source of something important for a coach to know. It may be the assistant offering strategy ideas or advice on how to handle a certain situation. It may be a player's friend or a janitor in the locker room who drops a comment on you about a player having a real problem. Hall of Fame college basketball coach, Mike Krzyzewski (2000), talks about this very situation in his book, *Leading with the Heart*. "Good ideas can come from anywhere and everywhere. And often, they may come from the people you least expect to have them" (p. 100). Communication may come from anywhere, but if the coach isn't listening, he'll never hear it.

However, a coach also needs to be able to shut out those around him or her, too. The coach needs to figure out what information is important and what isn't. Too often we as coaches harp on and beat ourselves up over information that is irrelevant or just plain bothersome. We need to listen and then move on. The best source of information surrounding your team is usually those who are within it, especially assistant coaches.

Assistant coaches bring a fresh perspective to many situations, and they are a valuable resource for a head coach. This is why assistant coaches need to feel that they will be listened to. Otherwise, the assistants will not offer as many ideas as they could. This could ultimately hurt the program. Assistant coaches need to be loyal to the head coach, but they shouldn't be "Yes men" or "Yes women." Assistant coaches need to feel that they can approach the head coach on any situation and be open and honest with the head coach without the head coach biting off their heads.

A coach needs to recognize that there are a variety of ways that a person may communicate to him or her, too. Therefore, s/he needs to learn to listen in a variety of ways. Certainly a coach needs to listen to the words of the person speaking. But the coach needs to look at how the person is speaking as well. Is the communicator bold, withdrawn, nervous, etc.? This will often say as much or more than the words themselves. Body language is very important. Coaches need to learn to read a person's body language. What does it say about the message that the person is trying to get across? A coach also needs to listen to the "why." Why is this person talking to me? What is his or her ultimate goal? Is there a hidden agenda? These are examples of listening to the "why."

One final comment on listening is that when someone, be it a player, a parent, an assistant, or someone else, tells you they don't understand, don't argue with them and tell them that they should understand. Work with them to clear up their confusion. Understand their confusion and embrace it even. Then try a new tactic to get them to understand what you are saying or what you want done. And don't be angry with them for their confusion, unless they were just not paying attention to you. Communication is an on-going two way street, and it is always changing. Keep working at it, and you will find yourself more successful at getting people to understand you.

If you need to improve your communication skills, there are a variety of books, audiotapes, videos, and classes to help you with this. A couple of resources for you to check out to find materials to help with these and many other elements of coaching can be found on my website, www.greatresourcesforcoaches.com and on the Proactive Coaching website, www.proactivecoaching .info. The nice thing about using sources like these is that while you will be helping yourself be a better coach, you will also help yourself in terms of communicating in all aspects of your life.

7 ❖ Fun & Winning/Losing

Why does a coach coach? Why do players play? Why do spectators watch? Ultimately, it goes back to when we first got involved in sports. We do this because it is fun. However, as we get older, we sometimes lose track of the fun involved. It becomes more work than anything else. We have playbooks to memorize, early morning practices, conditioning, weight lifting, nutritional needs, long road trips, pressures from families of players, pressures from administration, pressures from ourselves, etc.

We can forget that it is a game. Games are meant to be fun. But with youth sports, there is a fine line between fun in sports and fun and games. There can be no room for goofing off, horseplay, or bullying and laughing at other kids, which are all things that kids sometimes feel is fun.

Sports have a fun that is often unique to the individual sports themselves. I see nothing fun about running two miles or swimming twenty laps, but I have friends who find absolute joy in those things. Somewhere along the way, they found that to be enjoyable. Those same people may not find working out in a weight room or playing three-on-three basketball enjoyable, but there are few things that I enjoy doing more than those things. So fun in sports is different for everyone. In team sports, this is where a coach comes in to help establish what is fun.

I believe a coach needs to teach kids what fun in sports is. One simple idea to get across to kids is that being good is fun. Improving your skills to a point that you are a good player and your team is a good team will lead to a lot of fun within your given sport. A huge part of this is practice. Practice is the most important part of a season, and it is the most important element in the development of an athlete. Players need to learn that it's fun to practice hard, to improve, and to be part of a team.

Drills need to be demanding, but there also needs to be some enjoyment sprinkled in as well. For instance, in basketball, if all we do for forty-five minutes is get into defensive stances and slide and take charges, and we never get the ball and "play," that would be no fun. Turning drills into contests and competition can create enjoyment, while at the same time being demanding and creating good work habits.

But even this needs to be monitored because soon all the kids will want to do is play games instead of learning necessary skills. Soon too, they will focus only on the contests and not on the other drills. All of this is dealt with by the coach taking time to create an effective practice plan. This is one reason why it is critical that coaches recognize the importance of good practice plans.

Another aspect of fun comes in the games. The games are why we decide to play in the first place. However, many players often feel that when it comes to games, the only way to have fun is to win the game. Players need to see that fun isn't only in winning or scoring. We need to show them that fun comes from putting forth maximum effort with a group of teammates to achieve some shared goal. Yes, it is more fun to win than to lose, and they need to see that, too. That helps instill a competitive drive. But if you feel it's only fun when you win, you may miss out on a lot of enjoyment during a sports career.

There is always a winner and a loser. If you define fun only based on winning and losing, there is always someone who has fun and someone who doesn't. I think that is far too limited in scope. Some of the most enjoyable, memorable games I was ever involved in were games in which we lost. Yes, I would have enjoyed them more at the end and since then if we had won. But it didn't diminish the joy of the game itself during the game. When you lose, you always look back and think, "What if…?" That's good because it forces you to be better prepared the next time. It is how losing can be a great teacher.

To want to win is an important part of athletics. To deserve victory is a key as well. These two things need to be taught to young players. But to teach them that winning is the only way to have fun in athletics is a mistake. We need to show them that there are numerous elements that make athletic competition fun. Also, we need to lead by example in this respect. If we tell them that there is more to enjoyment of the game than just winning, then we better not act like the world just ended every time we lose a game.

There is nothing wrong with being down and upset after a loss. In fact, it is good for kids to not enjoy and accept losing. But we need to teach kids how to deal with loss in a mature way. Teach them to learn from their losses, so they can go out and get better before the next game. That is just as important as teaching them about wanting to win. By yelling at kids after every loss and then telling them, "Not a word on the bus ride home!" we are really missing the point. No, we don't want them to be goofing around and playing games on the bus after a loss. But kids are extremely resilient, and they bounce back quickly and well. We as coaches could learn a bit from them in this respect.

Still, I know there are coaches out there who right now are thinking, "I hate when kids start talking or playing music after a loss as if nothing happened." I agree, and that's why I say we don't want to allow them to act like they just won. But we do need to strike a balance between losing and getting over the loss with moving on and turning things back around before the next game.

Ironically, this situation doesn't only happen when we lose. I once saw a show on TV where a camera crew was following a high school football team around for the season. I love watching these types of shows because I love to watch how other coaches coach. Now in defense of the coach of this particular team, I didn't see the whole episode. Also, from what I could gather, this was a very successful program that he had coached for awhile. But I had some problems with some of his tactics. The one I want to focus on here is a situation where the team won their game even though they did not play well. After the game, in no uncertain terms, he made it very clear to the team how disappointed he was in them. And since they played so poorly, even though they won the game, there was to be no talking on the bus ride home.

Now I know that there can be some games where we play poorly, still win the game, and we as coaches don't feel good about it. There is nothing wrong with letting your team know that they didn't play well, that they were lucky to come away with a win, and that you as the coach are not happy with the way the team played. But to make them not talk on the bus ride home, in my opinion, is going way overboard in that scenario. Again, in that coach's defense, I wasn't there, so I don't know all the extenuating circumstances. It's one of the reasons I don't like to criticize specific coaches when I haven't seen all that surrounded a situation. However, from what I saw on the camera, I disagree with the way that coach handled that situation.

When we focus only on winning or being successful, it can lead to some problems with staying true to why we coach athletics. Coaches need to focus on improvement, development, teamwork, and camaraderie, along with winning the game. These are the things that make coaching as important as it is, yet we as coaches sometimes need to be reminded of that.

8 ❖ Treatment of Players

When it comes to coaching, there is probably nothing more important than how coaches treat players. Some words that come to mind when thinking about treatment of players are: respect, discipline, caring, compassion, fair, consistent, accountable, demanding, honesty, listening, and positive. While this is not a complete list, nor is it in any particular order, each of these words indicates something a coach needs to focus on when dealing with kids.

Respect—A coach needs to respect players. Coaches need to recognize that players make mistakes, have weaknesses, struggle with certain things, and have their own goals and reasons for playing. A coach needs to respect the players' lives away from the sport. There must be a healthy respect for the uniqueness of each individual on the team. At the same time the individual athlete needs to respect the team and all that it entails. It is up to the coach to work to instill this in his players.

Discipline—Respect is something that is so important in our lives, yet it is difficult to ensure that it is part of the equation. That is where discipline comes into the picture. Coaches need to instill discipline in the individuals on their teams, so that they maintain respect for all of the elements around them that are a part of that team and the sport. Without discipline, it is hard to create and maintain the kind of respect necessary for a team to thrive.

Caring & Compassion—However, discipline needs to be instilled with caring and compassion. Kids need to know that their coaches and teachers care about them. If they are going to be told how to behave, that behavior needs to be modeled and reinforced by their coaches as well.

Fair & Consistent—The discipline that coaches instill in their teams must be fair and consistent. If coaches expect a rule to be followed, then they need to enforce it fairly and consistently. Coaches also need to make sure that they don't "take a night off" with regards to instilling and enforcing discipline. That is part of being consistent.

Accountable—When respect and discipline are instilled, enforced, and maintained, then coaches are on their way to making players accountable for their actions. Too often coaches mean well when it comes to these areas, but then they don't stick to it by holding their players accountable. When players are not accountable for their actions, the whole system breaks down, and the concept of "team" suffers. All that a team works for is thrown away at that point.

Demanding—Accountability for one's actions does not just occur, though. It must be demanded by the coaches. Coaches can't just say that this is what they want and expect that it is going to be that way. Demanding accountability is following up when players don't do what they are supposed to. It is coaches doing exactly what they say they will do, so the players will do the same. It's meaning "No," when saying "No." It's making sure that "team" comes before "individual" all the time, not just when it is easy.

Honesty—All of this can only be accomplished when there is honesty between coaches and players. Coaches need to be straight-up with players. They need to let players know where they stand. Honesty is critical, but it needs to be given with tact. To tell a player that he or she sucks would be honest, but it would not be tactful. In fact it would be downright hurtful. There is no place for this in the coach/player relationship. Remember caring and compassion. They must be a part of the honesty with which coaches express themselves.

Listening—Coaches need to do more than just tell players things; coaches need to listen to players as well. Listening is a huge part of communication. Coaches can learn a lot about a team and their players by listening to the members of the team. Sometimes it's not even the actual listening that is so important as much as the other person, in this case the player, knowing that he or she is being listened to.

Positive—All of this has to occur in a positive, upbeat atmosphere. As much as possible, coaches need to stay positive with their players. Of course, there are going to be times when coaches will not be able to be positive. But they need to constantly keep in mind that the more the players feel positive vibes from the coach, the more they will react in a positive manner. A team takes its cues from its coach, and a positive team is generally a more successful team.

Yelling

Does yelling have a place in kids' sports? I believe it does, but it needs to be done in certain ways, at certain times, for certain reasons. Now I'm sure that some people reading this are saying to themselves, "Oh, my. He says that yelling is okay." Yes, I do. Let's face it. Coaches are going to yell at kids. That's not going to stop, nor do I believe that it necessarily has to. My thinking is that if they are going to yell at kids, let's at least talk about the hows and whys and ways to yell. Hopefully then, it will be done in a manner that is more acceptable and more worthwhile. There is no place for the type of yelling that goes on in many athletic situations. But yelling can and does have its place.

Parents raise their voices at their kids all the time. Why can't a coach do the same while s/he has to deal with the same effort and attitude or lack thereof on the court or field for which a parent yells at his or her children at home? I think it is perfectly acceptable behavior if it is done properly, with good reason, and not too often. Following are some examples of acceptable and unacceptable yelling in more depth.

Reasons to Yell

First of all, let's look at why a coach may yell. Maybe the team needs a wake-up call. Maybe the players are arguing with each other and need to be broken up. Maybe they are just not playing with any heart or working very hard. Sometimes yelling at a team gets their attention. This is especially true if the coach does not yell too often. If a coach doesn't yell much and all of a sudden, he or she is yelling, the team will know that something serious is happening. However, a coach needs to have the respect of his or her players already in place, so that when the coach yells, the players don't shut the coach out, stop listening, or start laughing. This is accomplished by laying a solid foundation of discipline, caring, and respect from the first day.

On the other hand, if a coach is always yelling, then the yelling starts to lose its effect and its strength. Players just tune out the coach and think, "Here he goes again." This style of coaching has really become a turn-off to players in this day and age. Quite honestly, I'm glad. I'm all for instilling discipline, demanding hard work and accountability, and establishing and enforcing standards and rules. But there is no need for a coach to be a raving lunatic who is always launching into a tantrum. This behavior has given coaches a bad name, and it's time we say good-bye to it.

On the other end of the spectrum is the coach who never yells. If a coach can instill discipline, make kids accountable, and get them to play hard without ever having to yell, that's great. I want to meet this person and find out his or her method because I have never been able to go through a season without yelling at my team. I'm not a lunatic, but I do yell at them occasionally, sometimes a bit more than occasionally. (If any of my players or ex-players are reading this, right now they are saying, "Occasionally?!? Hah! That's a laugh." I will explain my yelling more when I talk about how and what to yell.) If a coach can go through a season without having to yell and still maintain control, focus, discipline, respect, and all other aspects of coaching, then I applaud that coach.

Now some coaches never yell, but their teams have no discipline, don't work hard, won't listen or focus, and/or have no respect for the coaches. This is a problem situation that must be changed. Often a coach is afraid to yell at the team for fear of the consequences. This is especially true when a coach has a player or players who are hard to handle. The coach may think, "If I can just avoid confrontation with the players, then everything will be okay." That is usually a set-up for future failure. When the coach finally has had enough, it is too late. This coach has lost his or her team. Yelling now probably won't get them back, but something has to be done.

Start over and instill the discipline, get them to work hard and listen, and demand their respect. Then if you do raise your voice at them, they will be less likely to laugh at you or blow you off. I found that both in the classroom and on the court or field, the earlier in a season that I had to raise my voice and "get after them" the better things went. It's like a quarterback getting hit for the first time in a football game. He doesn't necessarily want it to happen, but the longer it takes to happen, the more afraid of it he becomes and the more tentatively he plays. So, get that "first hit" in early in the season, and you will feel better about it the next time you have to do it.

Why You Shouldn't Yell

There are also times when a coach shouldn't yell. A coach should never yell at players without being in control of himself or herself. Otherwise things can be said that are damaging and hurtful, and it could create far more problems than it was worth. A coach should not yell at a team that can't handle it. Know your team. Know what they can and can't take. This goes for individuals, too. Some players can take being yelled at and some can't. You need to know who is more sensitive to being yelled at.

That doesn't mean you don't discipline. You just need to do it in other ways. But make sure the rest of the team knows this player is not being favored. They need to know that player is being held accountable, too. The concept of treating every kid exactly the same is a joke. They are not all the same and shouldn't be treated as such. However, they should all be treated consistently and fairly. You can treat kids individually while still maintaining all of your rules and your ability to be fair and consistent. You just have to figure out how to do it.

Let me give you an example. I once had two good post players on the same varsity basketball team who were very close friends. I will call one of them Dave and the other one Tim (not their real names).

Dave was a kid who the best way to motivate him was to yell at him, and he told us so. Some kids are like that. They know that when they need to get going, the best way for them to turn it around is to have someone get on them and yell at them. As a young coach, I was happy to oblige Dave.

But Tim was a different personality. He was a very good player, but he just could not handle the yelling the same way as his friend could. With Tim, you needed to pull him aside and explain to him what he had done wrong and how to correct it. I had to make sure, though, that everyone else saw that Tim was still being corrected or disciplined, depending upon the situation. And if it was in practice on the floor, I would often start by yelling out, "Tim!" and then making my way over to him or pulling him out of a drill to explain to him what the mistake was and the proper way to fix it.

The rest of the team heard the initial, "Tim!" in a raised voice and knew he was not getting away with something that they couldn't get away with either. But Tim did not have to stand out there in front of his friends and teammates and feel bad about himself and go into a shell, which is what used to happen before I figured out that I couldn't treat Tim the exact same way as I could other players. It took me years to figure this out, and Dave and Tim were instrumental in helping me do so. They were great teachers to me about the importance of always treating kids individually, but fairly.

Another time not to yell is when a team's confidence is low. If a team is in a slump and they are doubting themselves, that's the time they need to hear more positive things than anything else. They need to know that you believe in them, that they will get through this, and that they are good players. Conversely, when a team is on a roll and feeling good about themselves, you can be a little tougher on them.

Finally, NEVER yell at a team of kids who are too young to understand it. Who am I talking about? Grade school and youth teams in the kindergarten through 5th or 6th grade would fall into this category. Why do you feel the need to yell at third graders who are just learning the game and trying to find themselves within it?

Now this doesn't mean that we don't instill discipline, focus, sportsmanship, teamwork, and respect. No, it is precisely at these younger grades that all of those things need to be taught. It's just that we don't have to yell at our teams to do that.

You may raise your voice to get a point across, but you don't have to yell at them. Find other ways to enforce your rules, such as sitting a player down off to the side, pulling a player aside and sternly explaining why the behavior is inappropriate, or sitting a kid on the bench who is not behaving properly during a game. You must address the behavior. Just do it without yelling at the kids. As players get a little older, then you can start to use yelling as a method to get your point across. But I wouldn't do so until kids were into the middle school years, and even then it would be done very sparingly.

If we teach kids the rules and enforce them fairly, firmly, and consistently, then we shouldn't have to yell at them too much. Then as they get older, they will be that much better at behaving appropriately in an athletic setting. Also, if you coach at an older level (varsity in high school, for instance) and you have what would be considered a "young team" of many freshmen and sophomores, you generally don't want to yell at this team too much. They have a fragility to them when they are learning how to compete at that level, and good coaches know they need to pick and choose wisely when they do and do not yell at their team.

How Do You Yell?

So how does one yell at a team? There is no guidebook on this. As I said before, though, if you are yelling without being in complete control of yourself, you are setting yourself up for real problems. Always maintain your control while yelling at a team. Also, stick to the point. Be specific. If you are sick of their poor practice habits, and that is why you are yelling at them, don't start in on something else, unless of course it is related to the poor practice habits. If this yelling incident is during practice, one way is to blow the whistle and get their attention by yelling, "HEY!!" Then start in on them. However, don't go on for too long. Make your point, and get on with practice. If you are going to kick them out of practice (and this is occasionally a very effective move), then kick them out and tell them to make sure they leave immediately, and they better be ready to go the next day. Then make the next day a very demanding, physically difficult practice. They will remember this for a long time, and it will help to bring practice habits back up to par.

In games, keep in mind that the whole gymnasium may be watching you. While you shouldn't let that stop you from coaching and getting on your team, keep in mind that people are watching and listening to you. Parents can be very sensitive about how you treat their child. Also, keep in mind there are young children watching the game, some sitting very close to you. Keep your cool, even when you are getting hot.

And by all means watch your language. Some people feel that swearing is a part of athletics. Who says it has to be? Don't get me wrong. I have sworn around and at my teams before. I realize now that there was no need for it, and I should have handled myself differently. Also, just like yelling, if it is done to excess, it loses any effectiveness it may have. Also, some people are far more sensitive to it than others, and you may be called on it. This is especially true at the school and youth level. I personally feel that you can get your feelings across just fine without having to swear, and the athletes don't need to hear you swearing at them.

Remember that you are setting an example. You want your team to exhibit good sportsmanship and to be good ambassadors of your school. What kind of an ambassador are you? Think about it. At younger grades, there is never any excuse for a coach to swear. Younger players don't need to think that this is how athletics are going to be for their whole lives. They will hear other players swear enough as it is. They don't need to hear you doing it, too. And when I am talking about swearing, I am referring to just about any word that can be deemed a swear word, not just the "biggies."

What Do You Yell?

Along with *how* a coach yells at his team is *what* a coach yells at his team. The fact that you raise your voice when communicating to them is not a problem. The problem comes into play based on what you are saying when you yell at them along with how you say it. Earlier, I alluded to my players laughing if they were to hear me saying that I occasionally yell at them. I was referring to the concept of actually yelling at them about poor behavior, habits, play, etc. I do not do that a lot.

More than anything, when I yell, I am yelling instructions or some kind of positive, supportive statement. It is not always easy to be heard in a gym for a varsity basketball game, so I often have to yell. That's the nature of team sports. But there certainly are times in a game when I yell at a specific player or the entire team because of poor behavior, like not working hard or being selfish or lazy. Sometimes, the only way to point those types of things out and get a change in behavior is to yell at them.

So is there a place for yelling? I believe there is. But it needs to be done the right way and at the right times.

9 ❖ Inappropriate Behavior

Touching

Obviously, a lot of things could fall under a category of "Inappropriate Behavior." The first place I want to focus on is touching kids. Now right off the bat, most people are thinking about that statement in a sick, demented, sexual way. That's a shame, but that's the world we live in today. Certainly, touching a kid in that way or having an inappropriate relationship with a kid falls into this category, and it is an issue that must be dealt with.

But you don't need me to tell you that such behavior is wrong. Coaches who do this are lawbreakers, and they need to be removed from the teaching/coaching situation and be put in jail. Unfortunately, we continue to read and hear about this all too often. We have a lot of work to do with regards to background checks, holding coaches accountable, and continuing education for coaches, so that these types of law-breakers do not continue to destroy kids' lives.

In 2004 the Seattle Times ran a four-day article on this issue, just in the state of Washington. The story pinpointed numerous coaches who had coached on a variety of levels who had been accused and often found guilty of such behavior. The scariest thing was how many of them were still coaching at the time the article was written. The most bothersome aspect of that was that in exchange for them leaving their original school district, the school districts agreed not to disclose to other school districts the reasons for their removal. That means that school districts knowingly allowed people who had acted in the most despicable way with a young person to turn around and go work with young people again, as long as it wasn't with young people in their district! That is unacceptable. We are either in this for all kids, or we aren't. We in the education and coaching world should not be in it for our kids only.

The Fine Line of Touching Kids

While we know that inappropriate touching and relationships with kids is wrong, let's talk about other forms of touching kids. Here is the problem and the fine line that we walk with regards to this. Touching kids used to be completely acceptable. In fact, it was in many ways a big part of athletics. From the consoling arm around the shoulder to the either gentle or not-so-gentle pat on the backside, coaches used touch as a way of helping their communication and creating a bond with their players. And it was not done in such a way that people said, "That's creepy." It was just a part of the game.

Nowadays, coaches have to be very careful about how they touch kids. Most of the time, you will hear people say, "Don't ever touch a kid." We have gotten to a point where no one trusts anyone anymore. What a shame. While I don't subscribe to the "never touch a kid" theory, I get why some do, and I totally understand their feeling. However, I still will put my arm around a player's shoulder when he or she needs that. But no matter what sex you coach, you must be careful.

For instance, no matter who I am coaching, I don't pat them on the rear end anymore. When I coached varsity girls' basketball, I would sometimes tap a girl on the leg or knee when she was sitting next to me, and I wanted her to go report into the game. Or I would do the same thing when she had just come out of the game, and I wanted her to know she did a good job or she needed a little consoling for having a tough time out there.

The point is touching is something people have done for thousands of years to help them communicate with one another. In the last thirty years with more and more cases of child abuse and molestation coming to the forefront, we have decided that it is wrong. Well, touching players appropriately isn't wrong. Unfortunately, every time you do it, you run the risk of being labeled a sexual predator, and your entire career is on the line.

So it is up to each coach individually to determine whether he or she wants to run that risk. If you are going to touch players in some positive, acceptable fashion, you must first establish a positive relationship with them. If you have a good relationship with them, then touching them in this way can end up being an almost natural extension of the relationship. We high-five and fist-bump players all the time. That is a form of touching. So the arm around the shoulder, the tap on the knee or the top of the head can all be positive forms of touch in the player/coach relationship. But it all starts with making sure that that relationship is a good one.

I am confident that my kids have known me well enough to know that I only mean to help them with such behavior, but in the back of my mind, I have also worried. What has kept me doing it is knowing that I am doing nothing wrong, and I am doing it in an up-front and appropriate fashion.

While I was coaching girls' basketball, I once asked a female athletic director about this situation. She told me I shouldn't worry. She said, "I know you, and I've seen you coach. I'm sure your girls look at you as if they are looking at their dad. It is completely healthy and acceptable." That made me feel good.

Still, I'm sure there is someone reading this who is saying, "That's what I thought. And they kicked me out of coaching for it." That's what scares me. I think that ultimately, you live with yourself, and you look yourself in the mirror each night. If you can look in the mirror and know in your heart that you did nothing wrong, that's got to be the most important thing. Unfortunately, there may be a great coach who is great for kids who is sitting out there today who did nothing wrong but who is not allowed to work with kids anymore, or worse yet, sitting in jail. That is a travesty.

Hitting/Grabbing Kids

Another form of touching kids is hitting them. This one is without a doubt a no-no. There is never, ever a time when smacking a kid is appropriate behavior, unless the kid is coming after you and you are defending yourself. Hitting kids is wrong; there is no room for argument here. However, what constitutes hitting a kid is where the debate occurs. Let me give some examples.

In a football game, a player misses a block for the third time in a row. You pull him out of the game. As you are in his face and explaining to him the errors of his ways, he keeps staring out into space past you. You grab his face mask to jerk his head back so that he can look you in the eyes, and you say, "Look at me when I am talking to you!" Inappropriate?!? Maybe, especially if it is the President of the school board's kid.

How about this one? You take your "star" player out of the basketball game because she has just committed her fourth turnover in two minutes. She had not liked how you challenged her to step up her play during the last time out. As she walks toward you and you put your hand out to "give her five," you are starting to talk to her. She snubs the high-five and keeps walking toward the end of the bench. You grab the back of her jersey to stop her from continuing to the bench and to turn her around, as you say, "I'm not done talking to you yet." Inappropriate?!? Maybe, especially because it is so visible in a gymnasium with 400 people in it. Also, if you are a male, it could be a lot worse than if you are a female.

So here's the dilemma. I think both of these situations are perfectly acceptable if they are done properly. If there is no screaming, the jerk or the grab is not done too violently, and the physical touch lasts for no more than a second, it seems to me to be perfectly within the bounds of a coach's rights. However, I am a coach, not an attorney. And in this sue-happy world in which we live, both of these cases are causes for huge problems for these coaches.

In fact, each of these scenarios happened to two different coaches I know. Neither coach was coaching at that school the next year. They didn't get sued over the situations, but life was made miserable enough for them that they decided it was time to go elsewhere. The shame is that each of them may be asked to justify it in the future as they try to get another coaching job. I wasn't there, so I don't know exactly how either situation went. Neither were the people who will interview these coaches. So we now formulate an opinion of these coaches based upon "their" version of what happened.

As an Athletic Director and one who interviewed potential coaching candidates all the time, I was often wary of a coach who told me this kind of a story. And as I said earlier, if it was done properly, in my opinion, there would be nothing wrong with both situations. However, not having seen it, and only getting the coaches' perspectives on the situations, it would be hard to not take it into consideration in the hiring process, especially if someone with similar credentials is interviewing who has no incident on his or her record (that we know of).

The bottom line is that if you do touch a student/ athlete, you always run the risk of it coming back and hurting you in the end. However, even if you don't touch a kid, you could still have accusations leveled at you that you did or that you acted inappropriately in other ways. That being the case, I choose to do what I have always done: put my arm around kids' shoulders when they need it, tap them on the leg to acknowledge a good play or to signal to go in the game, and or give a consoling pat on the knee when they need some comforting words. I know in my heart that when I touch a kid, I am doing nothing wrong. If I get accused of wrong-doing, and I can't prove my innocence, I will have to live with it. But I am not going to change my style, which has been successful and very well-received, because of the fear that someone may attack me.

Teachers have continually been losing their ability to really nurture and help young people in the last thirty years because of this. It is a shame, and I for one am not going to change something that I know works and is perfectly innocent and acceptable. You, however, will have to make that decision for yourself.

Ethics & Cheating

Another form of coaches' inappropriate behavior deals with ethics, specifically, cheating to win. The profession of coaching is one that needs to be approached and handled with the highest degree of ethics. Sports are all about competing fairly. When one walks out onto a field of play, s/he should be able to expect that the playing field is level and that he or she will be treated fairly. Unfortunately, all too often it doesn't work this way. However, participants should be able to expect that it will work this way. It is up to all of us to work to make this happen.

Coaches play a large role in the ethics of the game. In fact, when it comes to ethics in the game, they probably play the largest role of all those involved. And yet, time and time again, we hear stories of or complaints of coaches acting in unethical and unprofessional manners. Sometimes the unethical behavior can be something that seems minor, like stealing signs in a baseball game. While it is not the worst thing a coach can do, it is unethical. Or it can be a basketball coach who has a player get fouled who is a bad free throw shooter, so the coach tries to have another player step to the line to shoot the free throws. The coach is telling his players that you do whatever you have to do to win, no matter if it is wrong. Doing anything that bends the rules in your favor in order to gain an advantage is pushing the boundaries of ethical behavior for coaches.

Ethics & Illegal Recruiting

Another area of coaches exhibiting unethical behavior is illegally recruiting kids to play for their team. Illegal recruitment of kids is a huge issue at the high school level. It has been a huge issue for a long time in states all across the country. I remember it being an issue in Illinois when I was growing up in the 70's and coaching in the 80's, and it is still an issue in the western states where I have lived since the 1990's. Some people will often point to it being a public school vs. private school issue. However, we have seen all kinds of situations where it has occurred in every type of school imaginable. We could pinpoint numerous stories of illegal recruitment, but one in particular in 2006 when I was an athletic director and coach in the state of Washington was kind of a poster child for the problem.

An article appeared in the *Seattle Times* online newspaper that year with strong allegations about a girls' varsity basketball coach illegally recruiting. The evidence against him was overwhelming. The team was 3-17 during the four years prior to the new coach taking over. All kinds of incredible players started showing up over the next four years. Within two years the team was in the state tournament, and they were the state champions the next two years, going undefeated in the fourth year.

Many players, former players, and parents of former players who claimed to have been recruited by the coaches stepped forward to tell their stories. Promises of playing time and college scholarships, offers to provide fake apartment/home leases to kids who lived outside of the school district, and a deal on a car for a kid who lived far away were all part of the accusations. This coach went way out of line to build his dream team, and he was eventually fired, and his team had to forfeit all their games and their championships.

This story points to a huge issue in ethics in youth sports. This coach acted in an extremely unethical manner. What lessons did he teach young people:

- If you cheat the rules and the system, you will have a better chance at winning.

- Don't worry about the rules; they can be manipulated to make things work for you.

- All that matters at the end of the day is that you win.

Are these the lessons that we want our kids learning from our leaders? What about fair play, integrity, honesty, making the most of the situation you are in, and working hard to overcome adversity? Oh, I'm sure he worked hard to overcome the situation at his school. He just worked hard at illegally recruiting kids to do it, instead of working hard with the hand he was dealt. There is no place for this kind of unethical behavior in athletics, especially at the levels where we are trying teach our youth the kinds of lessons that will carry them through life.

Hopefully, this coach didn't scar so many kids who went

through his program or watched his program. Hopefully, most of them realize that this was wrong, and that he needed to be punished for it. Unfortunately, there are some people who see nothing wrong with it and who feel that everything is just fine. I worry that we will be reading about these kids in another article someday in the future when they do something similar in terms of unethical behavior. A coach has a huge amount of impact on a child's life. We as coaches must always remember that and act accordingly.

10 ❖ Playing Time & Cuts

Without a doubt, the biggest issue that coaches have to deal with parents on is playing time. It has gotten so bad that many coaches have written into their policy sheet for their sport that they will not talk to parents about playing time. While I don't agree with that position, it does underline the problem. Coaches need to have a playing time philosophy, and they need to communicate that philosophy to their players and their parents. My ideas on playing time issues and philosophies follow.

Younger Ages/Levels

At lower levels of play (youth sports through Junior Varsity), all kids should be getting good amounts of playing time. Notice I didn't say equal amounts of playing time. You will rarely have equal amounts of playing time unless you substitute based on the clock, and every kid gets four or five minutes at a time, no matter what the game situation is. For very young kids this is fine. You may not want to use a scoreboard then, because you aren't focused on winning in that situation.

When kids start getting up around the fifth and sixth grade though, things change. Competition is more important. This is a great age to teach what is truly important. Yes, we keep score. But we don't make the final score the ultimate determinant of success and enjoyment. Everyone needs to play, and everyone needs to play a decent amount of time.

It is also good to have kids play numerous positions in order to learn numerous roles on the team. This will help them have a greater appreciation for the other players and what they go through, as well as help them with their own development. A fifth grader has no clue what position s/he will end up in later in life if s/he stays with the sport. The more positions s/he has played, the better prepared s/he will be.

Middle School

The older a child gets, the more specialized the child can get and the more the playing time issues change. In middle school, kids should still be getting a good mixture of decent amounts of playing time, but the players with better ability need to start playing a bit more. That is because you are also developing a whole program, and the players who are going to have the greatest impact down the road are the ones who have more ability. So they need to get more time. Still, they shouldn't play a grossly inordinate amount of time compared to the other kids, but they should be out there more.

One way to help with this is by having "A" teams and "B" teams and so on if your league allows you to do so. That way you can have the kids with more ability playing together against kids with similar ability. If, however, you don't have the ability to split your teams up, then you must try to get all of the kids a good amount of time, while getting the better kids the most time.

This is where things start to get sticky for a coach and parents. It's not easy to determine what exactly is "grossly inordinate." Also, it can't only be about ability. Attitude, work ethic, school behavior, etc. all must play a role in a kid's playing time. The bench is one of the greatest teachers for a coach to use. It is the coach's equivalent of a parent "grounding" a child. "If you don't do _____, you will sit," or "If you do _____, you will sit." So a coach has to use this as a teaching tool for the entire team. This goes for all ages by the way, from the youngest to the oldest. It's just that at the youngest ages, you sit them for a very short time and get them back in.

High School

At the high school level, playing time becomes the big focus. As I said earlier, the largest amount of complaints that coaches receive from parents are about playing time. While parents are usually way off base with this and are often quite unrealistic about their kids' abilities, coaches are not infallible when it comes to making mistakes with regards to kids' playing time. Coaches need to recognize the level at which they coach and the goals for that level. A coach at the varsity level needs to deal with playing time differently than all the other levels. The major focus of the lower levels is to develop kids for the varsity level. So those kids must all be getting some decent amount of playing time.

If you have a "no-cut" policy at your school, then this can be very difficult. I don't believe in "no-cut" policies at the high-school level, but many schools have them. I think you invite many more problems by having a "no-cut" policy. At the middle-school level and below, a "no-cut" policy is great. But when kids start getting to high school, it is time to let them know that either A) they really don't have the skills necessary to succeed at this sport at this time, or B) they must behave according to the rules and standards that have been established, or they cannot be a part of the program.

Cutting Kids

Cutting kids is one of the hardest things a coach has to do and a player has to go through. But it is quick pain, much like ripping a Band-aid off a cut. It hurts a lot, but it is over. Keeping a kid on the team who then never plays is a slow pain that you both deal with every day. It is trying to take that band-aid off millimeter by millimeter because you don't want to have to deal with the potentially big pain. You are far better off dealing with a large amount of pain all in one fell swoop than a little bit everyday of the season.

I have done it both ways, and I know from experience that the pain of cutting a kid hurts immensely. But the next day, you move on, and you deal with your team, and you build your season. The kid also moves on. It obviously hurts her/him more and longer, but s/he, too, eventually gets over it. Some will come back out again in the future. Some will even make it in the future. Most won't, however. Again, when dealing with the high school age, this is the time to start telling them that their skills are not where they need to be in order to play on the team.

After you cut the kid though, it's still not over. Now the parent will want to meet. That's fine. After all, you just did the equivalent or worse of giving an "F" to a kid in class. If a student gets an "F" in a class, we expect that the parent is going to want to know why. The same will go if the child gets cut from the team. So it is up to coaches to talk to the parents to explain why their child just didn't have what it takes to make the team.

However, in class, a teacher can point to failed tests and quizzes or no homework handed in or other tangible elements. In sports, it is much harder to pinpoint why a player got cut, and this is where the sticking point can occur. Dad thinks that Junior shoots the ball great. In the coach's estimation, Junior is a decent shooter, but Junior is a point guard. This team already has three shooting guards who shoot better than Junior, and they all play good defense, and two of them are better ball-handlers. Each of these ideas is subjective. There is no concrete evidence to back them up.

Actually, many coaches have gone to grading tryouts, so they have something more tangible to be able to use to back up their decisions. In fact, many coaches who use a grading system will tell you they actually make their decisions based upon the point totals. I would be hesitant to do that, and I question how many coaches pick their teams based on a test score. There is still something to be said for intangibles and gut feelings. How about the attitude that the kid displays? She is always the first to show up and the last to leave. She addresses you politely and looks you in the eye when she speaks. She is always encouraging her teammates. Her grades are outstanding. Conversely, you also have players who are the exact opposite. Those types of things are all part of what goes into a coach's thought process when determining her or his team, especially the last few spots.

So it is a difficult process. When a parent comes in to talk about it, it is up to the coach to maintain a calm and understanding manner, no matter how the parent acts. The coach needs to do her or his best to explain as many tangible elements as possible that s/he can. S/He must focus on skills that the child was lacking. If there are attitude issues, the coach may want to mention them, but this is not always advisable. Attitude is so much more subjective and personal that it can lead to more problems. If the kid talked back or refused to do something, then the coach can talk about those things because they are tangible. But to just say, "Well, Junior has a bad attitude," says very little to the parent.

For more on the issue of playing time and cuts, check out my booklet, *Playing Time: Guidelines for Coaches, Athletes, and Parents* at www.greatresourcesforcoaches. com.

11 ❖ Sportsmanship

Ultimately, when I think of the role of the coach, instilling proper sportsmanship is one thing that should be at the top of the list of what a coach is there to do. Yes, we all want to win games, and yes, our fans want to see the team win and have great success. However, when it comes to our youth sports, if we win a lot of games and we have poor sportsmanship, then we have lost. There is no more important lesson that we teach our kids through athletics than how to be a "good sport."

Unfortunately, poor sportsmanship is running rampant these days at all levels of sports. From the pros on down to youth leagues, we see people behaving in terrible ways. This goes for the players, the coaches, the parents, and the fans. Nobody is immune from the disease of poor sportsmanship. In the last thirty years, we have seen a huge decline in the way people involved in sports act. Why? What has happened?

Well, a big part of it is a societal thing. Our society has lost touch with basic tenets of civility and treating each other with respect. As people continue this downward spiral of civility, the sports that our kids play have been affected. Whether it be the coaches, parents, or the kids themselves, the games our kids play have been compromised by the way people behave on the field, on the bench, and in the stands. This one will take the longest time to change, as there are so many different people involved in it, and there are so many different ways and degrees that people behave poorly. But coaches have as much responsibility in this realm as anybody.

Our Obsession with Winning

Within our sports specifically, the whole emphasis on winning has changed. People have gotten so wrapped up in their sports that it has put huge pressures on people to feel that their team must win the game. Just look at the build-up and the hype for the Super Bowl or any other championship in professional and college sports. It is all about who will win the big game. Nobody feels that pressure more than the coaches of the teams.

Now let's bring that down to our youth and school-aged sports. We still see the same attitude prevalent, but just on a smaller scale. The level of intensity and excitement for winning the game and the championship is the same, though. People are coming out to games in droves, painting their faces, wearing shirts, carrying signs, yelling and screaming at officials, and getting caught up way too much in the winning and losing of games.

As an athletic director for twelve years, my biggest concerns were always how fans would act at games. I was always worried about what idiot I would have to address or even throw out of a game due to bad behavior, usually due to something that affected their team's chance of winning the game. Our attention in youth athletics has really shifted away from good sportsmanship and moved to winning games. It is up to us as coaches to work to bring that shift back. But how do we do that?

The Coach's Role in Sportsmanship

There is no one in the athletic world who has more control over sportsmanship issues than the coach. While they can't control all the idiot fans out there, they can control themselves and their players. It is up to the coaches to make good sportsmanship a top priority. I would never tell coaches that they need to make sportsmanship their only priority. I would also never say that winning isn't a priority. Of course it is. But winning should never supplant good sportsmanship, discipline, teamwork, work ethic, and these types of things as the #1 priority.

We have all seen teams that win games that we would never want our kids to play on because of the behavior that we have seen allowed to happen. That behavior is the direct responsibility of the coaches, and it is up to them to turn it around, or it is time to get out of coaching. There is no place for poor sportsmanship.

Four C's of Good Sportsmanship

But what exactly are good and bad sportsmanship, and how can a coach control them? It's funny, but sportsmanship is one of those things that is difficult to define, but you know it when you see it. That goes for good sportsmanship, and it goes for bad sportsmanship. The whole focus of good sportsmanship, though involves playing the game with four "C's": caring, compassion, class, and character. Good sports have a caring attitude. They "care" for their teammates, coaches, opponents, officials, fans, and the sport itself. They have "compassion" for their teammates as well as their opponents when things don't go so well for either of them. They show "class" in all aspects of the game, from being a gracious winner to not being a poor loser. And they live with great "character" by always acting in a manner that shows they have dignity and integrity. Coaches need to reinforce these positive qualities and emphasize them to their players.

At the same time coaches need to live by these qualities themselves. Their words and actions say it all, especially their actions. When we sit in the stands at a game, we often don't hear what the coach is saying, but we sure can see how he is acting. When a coach is constantly yelling at officials or is getting in someone's face, we have an idea as to what is going on, even though we don't know what is being said. A coach has to watch his own actions to make sure that he is maintaining his own level of good sportsmanship. After all, his kids take his lead. If he is not living by the four "C's," how can he expect his kids to be?

So *how coaches communicate* is as important, or even more important, than *what* they are actually saying. Ranting and raving on the sideline about a bad call is not going to change things. Just make your point, express your disagreement and dissatisfaction, and move on. Remember, your kids and your fans are watching you. Then, after the game, don't dwell on a bad call or poor officiating. It's part of the game, just like you not subbing a kid at the right time or your kid kicking a ball over the goal at a critical time are both parts of the game. Handle it with class. Your kids and your team will be better because of it.

On the flipside, when things are going very well, you need to show caring, compassion, class, and character as well. When you are playing against an obviously weaker team, there is no point in running up the score and demoralizing the opponent. There is no place in athletics for humiliating kids. Depending upon the sport, figure out what a comfortable lead is and start doing things to keep it from getting out of hand.

Handling Blowout Situations

Here are some things that coaches can do to limit the lead in a blowout situation. While each sport has its own unique elements, consider what might work along these lines for the specific sports you coach. First, figure out what a blowout margin is in your sport. As you achieve that margin, begin taking off any pressure type of play. When and how you do this will be impacted by what point in the game you are, as well as the ability of your opponent. When you have a weaker opponent, you can do this earlier in the game. However, with a better opponent where it just so happens to be your night and your opponent is struggling mightily, you might wait a bit longer to make that change.

Also, players who don't normally play as much need to be put into the game at that point. You don't necessarily have to put them all in together, especially in the earlier stages of the game, but they should definitely be worked into the game in some fashion. You can also put kids into positions that they aren't used to playing. As the difference in the score continues to climb, it is time to work on really slowing the game down and working on other things that your team needs work on. However, don't be working on things that will raise your margin of a lead too much.

All sports have their own versions of doing these things. In football, stop throwing the ball and don't do any trick plays. Put kids on defense that normally only play offense and vice versa. In soccer, switch goalkeepers and put your goal scorers on defense and your defenders on offense. It allows the goal scorers to see how hard those defenders work to get them the ball. Only allow scorers to try to score off of headers or only shooting the ball with the weaker foot. In baseball, change your lineup if you can. Put in a pitcher who needs some work and some confidence. Don't let your players steal or take extra bases on hits. In basketball, play subs, don't press, stop fast breaking, make multiple passes before shots (but don't play keep-away—that is more humiliating), and stop pressuring passes on wings. For your sport, figure out some of the same types of things to do to help keep things in check.

No matter the sport, the key is to recognize that we don't want to humiliate the opponent. I know the temptation is great to do this if they have done it to you in the past. But when you do that, all you are doing is stooping to their level. While you may be thinking that you are getting back at the coach for what was done to you in the past, you are not getting back at the coach. What you are doing is humiliating her or his players. The best lesson to try to teach is a lesson in class by not doing that to them. More importantly, you are trying to teach your own kids and everyone else watching the game that this is how one acts with true sportsmanship.

Unfortunately, we often hear stories of coaches who fail to understand this concept. I have seen too many football coaches who just kept pounding the ball into the end zone, or basketball coaches who keep fast breaking and pressing who end up winning by scores like 87–3, or soccer coaches keeping their best players in their normal positions while up 12–0 at halftime. (These are actual scores and situations from actual games played at the high-school level. In fact, a girls' basketball team in Texas established a new standard of poor sportsmanship a few years ago by beating an opponent 100–0!) Then the coaches try to justify their behavior by saying, "That's how we play the game. I'm not going to change what we are teaching our kids just because we have a big lead. It's up to the other team to do what they need to do to get better."

What a crock! Of course they need to get better. But how are they supposed to get better when they are being humiliated 100-0? It is time for you to get out of coaching right now, sir and madam. You are hurting the game, and you are hurting kids. There is no place for you in youth sports or high school sports. Go take your ego and your bad sportsmanship to the professional ranks where you can do whatever you want and not have to answer to anyone about it, which in and of itself, is also a crock. The professional levels SHOULD be the model of how all others do things. Unfortunately, lately I feel there is not too much that I want our school-aged kids taking from the professional ranks in terms of behavior and sportsmanship.

The Role of Professionals in Youth Sports Sportsmanship

This brings up another point. When are we going to start holding our professional coaches and athletes accountable in this regard, as well? Players and coaches at the youth level see these professionals acting in the most unsportsmanlike manners of all, and they feel that's how we are supposed to do it, too. I am tired of seeing young athletes imitating the unsportsmanlike and classless acts of the pros because they don't realize that it is wrong. For every great thing that some of the prima-donna superstars with great talent but poor sportsmanship can do on the field or court, they do infinitely more harm by their unsportsmanlike and unteam-like actions. Kids see them behave poorly and believe that if they do those things, they will get to the top. Phooey!! It's time to clean up the pros and the colleges, so that we can clean up our youth sports.

Let me finish this part of this section by highlighting an event that one athletic director called a "Funeral for Sportsmanship." In a basketball game during the season in which the article was written (2005–2006) a young girl from a high school in New York scored 113 points. That is a phenomenal accomplishment by one of the greatest high school players in the country at the time. That is, until you find out that the score of the game was 137-32. Epiphany Prince was the player; her coach was Ed Grezinsky, a veteran coach who had been very successful. Why did he keep her in the game? She had scored 59 points by halftime. Her previous career high had been 51 points, so she had already topped that. She only scored one free throw and four three pointers. Most of all of her other baskets were baskets against an incredibly weak team.

What a hollow record this is. Her coach should be ashamed of himself. His actions did nothing to help advance the game, kids in general, or even Epiphany Prince. In fact, in some ways he has hurt her because there are those out there who will feel more animosity towards her than anything else. After that performance, she could be considered a selfish prima-dona athlete who is only out there for her own points. Is that true? I don't know, but millions of people who read that article or saw that news story may feel that way. More importantly, all this "publicity stunt" did was humiliate and hurt the girls from the other team, as well as some of Epiphany's teammates.

Teach Your Players Good Sportsmanship

It is also up to coaches to teach players how to act in ways that demonstrate good sportsmanship. So what are some positive examples of players demonstrating the four "C's" in action? When a teammate struggles or has a bad game, a good sport is there to pick her up and tell her it's okay. She lets the teammate know that she still cares about her and that they will get through this together.

When an opponent gets knocked to the ground, a good sport helps her up and recognizes that, while they are opponents in this game, they are not enemies. They are both striving for the same thing, and they do so with mutual respect and admiration for one another. A good sport ALWAYS shakes hands with her opponent after the game no matter the outcome. She then praises the efforts of all involved and does not taunt, blame, or ridicule anyone.

Finally, a good sport lives with "character" by not only doing these things on the field of play, but by acting with caring, compassion, and class in the halls and classrooms at school, at the mall, in restaurants, at home, and everywhere else. A good sport truly walks the walk and talks the talk. Ironically, the best sports do this without you really realizing it because you don't hear them talking about it much, and you don't see them walking in such a way that brings attention to themselves.

So what does bad sportsmanship look like on a player? Bad sportsmanship comes in a variety of ways. It is a player trash-talking and taunting an opponent. It is a player making a good play and then calling attention to himself by pounding his chest or pulling out his jersey or whatever move that shows it is all about him. (I have no problem with players celebrating when big things happen in games, but doing it in an outlandish or selfish way is poor sportsmanship.) It is unnecessary and overly physical play. It is constantly complaining about calls by the officials or blaming officials for poor play. It is knocking an opponent down and not offering to help him up when you are right there. Or it is being knocked down and not accepting the offer of help up from an opponent. It is not shaking hands with an opponent after the game.

These are just a few of the ways that players can show poor sportsmanship within the game itself. Fortunately, most of the time nowadays in youth sports, the players themselves are not the poorest sports in the arena. They tend to handle themselves, for the most part, with the proper level of caring, compassion, class, and character.

It is up to coaches to continue to teach, instill, and foster good sportsmanship in their players. Ultimately, if coaches work hard to instill good sportsmanship in their teams, then they are doing what needs to be done to help our games become positive experiences again. While they won't be able to "change the world," coaches can make a difference by helping kids understand the right way to behave. Hopefully, other coaches will follow their lead and the lead that their teams show, and behave in such a way that all involved begin to understand what it means to be a "good sport."

12 ❖ Dealing with Officials

I would be remiss if I did not include some comments on officials in the chapter on coaches. While this section's focus is on coaches, officials are such a huge part of the game that we need to look at the dynamic between the two groups. Also, we need to take only a few minutes to talk about officials because they are really only a very small part of what we do. It's just that coaches and fans make them seem like a much bigger part of the equation.

We Need Officials

Officials are there to serve a purpose. They are there to administer the game and make sure that it is played fairly and safely. However, somewhere along the line, we as a sports society turned them into something far greater than that. They have now become the All-Powerful, All-Knowing, All-Seeing God that should never make a mistake with our children's games.

That is just preposterous. These people are merely there to help judge what goes on out in the competitive arena and make sure it is being done within the framework of the rules. Are they perfect? Of course not. Are they infallible? Ditto. They are flawed human beings who make mistakes just like you and me. They see things a certain way from their perspective, and they make a judgment about them. Sometimes we agree with the judgment and sometimes we don't. But to act as if they cannot make a mistake is a travesty.

When I first started coaching in the early 80's, I remember people saying that the best officiated games were ones when you didn't really notice the officials were there. Things ran smoothly and calls were made in such a way that it all made sense. Sitting here 30+ years later, I realize I haven't thought that way in a long time. And do you know why? It's not because the officials have changed; it's because the fans and coaches have changed. We have gotten to a point where we expect the official to be perfect or else we are going to "let him have it." Instead of watching the game to enjoy the game, many people watch the game and wait for the mistake, so they can pounce on the official and let him know he was wrong, and he sucks, and the fans aren't happy about it. What happened to make that be the way people view the games?

Well, there are a lot of answers to that question, some dealing with the game specifically and some dealing with society in general. But for our purposes here, let's focus on the game. People have come to take these games way too seriously. They are each a life and death experience, and doggone it, we just can't have any mistakes by the people in stripes. The players and the coaches can make mistakes all night long and be forgiven, but let an official make a mistake, and s/he will be ridden and ridiculed by the crowd for the rest of the night. One mistake creates a situation where now any call that goes against that crowd, good or bad, will mean harassment and verbal abuse for that official and often his or her partners. Why can't officials make a mistake? Why do we believe them to be perfect?

Coaches Set the Tone with Officials

Since this is the section on coaches, let me address the coaches' role in this situation. We as coaches have a huge role in helping this problem get turned around. While our fans don't always take our cue, when it comes to getting on officials, they quite often feed off of us. The time they feed off of the coaches the most is when the coaches are getting on the officials for a perceived bad call.

Let me try to illustrate it with a basketball scenario. We are in a tight game in a packed gym with two rival teams playing each other. Emotions are high. The game is a fast-paced one. A player drives to the basket and an opposing player steps in to try to take a charge. (By the way, this is the toughest call in all of basketball to make.) The official makes his call. One coach is happy; the other is livid. The coach who is livid jumps off the bench, screams, "No way!" and immediately meets the official at the scorer's table. He is yelling at the official, telling him that his kid was there and that it was a terrible call.

What he is saying doesn't matter nearly as much as how he is saying it. Gesticulating wildly, pointing his finger at the ref, and yelling loudly are all acts that his fans are seeing that show he believes it was a terrible call. They, in turn, feed off of that action. "Well, if coach saw it that way, then it must be right. We need to yell at the official, too, because we're right, and we're getting screwed." The official is human. He doesn't like to be called out and yelled at in front of hundreds of people. A thought like, "I'll show him," could spring to mind. "I'm the one in control of this game, not him." Now, the situation is even more highly charged, and the stage is set for some real coach, official, and fan problems.

Let's look at that situation with the coach handling it differently. The call is made. The coach gets up from his seat but doesn't jump and scream. He has his palms up in a pose that indicates, "What? How could you make that call that way?" As the official comes to the scorer's table the coach asks him if he can talk to him. The official steps over to him and side-by-side (not face-to-face) the coach says, "Didn't you think my guy was there?"

The official responds, "Coach, from my angle I saw your kid leaning in to try to get him. His feet were planted, but he slid his upper body over while the kid was in the air."

The coach says, "Gosh, it looked to me like he was there in great position."

"Maybe he was coach, but that's not how I saw it."

The coach says, "All right, but watch that closely, okay? We work on that every week."

"All right, coach. I will."

In this scenario, everything is said in a levelheaded tone. The coach is asking for an interpretation. The official is allowed to explain his view on it. It is not heated, and it sets a tone for the rest of the game that coach and official can work together here. Now the crowd may still be yelling and doing its thing. But it is not going to feed off the emotions and actions of the coach because there are none to feed off.

This is important to establish as a coach because there are other times when an official will make a call against a team, the coach can see it was the right call, but the crowd goes nuts. If the coach has maintained the proper demeanor described above, he may be able to help diffuse his crowd a bit by getting them to realize that maybe the official made the right call that time. You are always going to have idiots in your crowd who just plain feel that they are always right, and the official is always wrong, and it is their job to let the officials know that.

When I originally wrote this section a few years ago, I was thinking of a kid's parent at the school where I was coaching then, and I was thinking of when this parent was being himself. One time the parent started yelling about the call because a foul was called, and the parent thought it was on our kid. I could tell the official was calling the correct foul, and it was on the other team, but this parent was just up there talking and yelling about how the ref needed to open his eyes. I just turned around and looked at the parent, shook my head, and laughed as the official came to the scorer's table and announced the foul on the opposing player. The parent shut up pretty quickly at that point. The irony is that this parent was an official himself, or at least he was a part time official. It's funny though; I never saw him do any high school games, just youth and AAU games. I imagine he didn't want to deal with people like himself pointing out all his mistakes in a packed gym.

Unfortunately, we will probably always have these kinds of people at games. Until we, as an athletic community, stand up and say "Enough," then these morons will still be able to do what they do. Until then, we coaches need to help in the process by not inciting our fans to more unruly behavior by mimicking our unruly behavior.

Problem Officials

Now, here is one of the few problems that I do have with officials: when they, too, buy into the concept that they are infallible and can't make a mistake. I have known too many officials who feel that they are too good to talk to the coaches or carry themselves in such a way as to say, "Don't talk to me; I'm in control here." I have seen it in all three states in which I have coached, from the smallest schools to the biggest schools. The arrogance of some officials drives me crazy. Come on. You're refereeing a high school basketball game. Who do you think you are? You are here for kids, just as I am. They deserve your attitude to be the same as mine needs to be, that of a servant-leader. You're here for us; it's not the other way around.

And officials, please don't act like you can't make a mistake. If you make one, admit it and move on. In the heat of the moment, I may get upset when an official tells me he blew a call. Ultimately, I would much rather have that than the guy who will not even acknowledge my presence because I am questioning him on a bad call. I respect the official who after the game says to me, "Coach, I think you're right. I think I missed that double-dribble there on #12." I would rather he called it when it happened, but he didn't, and we as a team have to rise above that mistake.

Ultimately, that's all it was—a mistake by a human being. He was running down the floor with ten kids running as well, and he missed seeing something that one of those ten kids did. It's going to happen in sports, and we as coaches better figure that out and live with it, or we are going to be miserable people, always complaining about how someone else isn't perfect. So get over it, coaches. Figure it out. Officials are not the devil; they are human beings who make mistakes, but who are out there just like you and me—trying to help kids have a positive experience.

Conclusion to Coaches' Quarter

So these are some of the problems that we in the coaching world need to address. We need to work hard to improve at what we do. We need to continually upgrade our knowledge of our games, but more importantly, we need to upgrade our knowledge of coaching in general. Also, we need to always keep in mind that we are here to provide kids a positive experience, not the other way around. Obviously, it works in reverse, or we as coaches wouldn't do this for as long as we do. However, our enjoyment of the experience should be secondary to making sure that our kids have enjoyable experiences.

Also, the administrations of schools and youth leagues need to help coaches improve by providing opportunities for education about coaching and about their specific sports. We need to treat staff development for coaches the same as we treat staff development for teachers. We need to fund coaches' education for all levels of athletics. This may be the toughest part. However, without proper funding, education will not exist, and ultimately, good coaching will be tough to come by.

I would like to close this section on coaches with a quote from a commentary by Frank Deford, senior contributing writer to *Sports Illustrated*. His commentary was on the personal relationships that coaches establish with their athletes and how important those relationships are to the development of young people. After talking about the various roles that a coach assumes in a young athlete's life, Deford closed his commentary by saying, "Coaches make vital impressions on our children. Never forget, for whatever reason, they are hugely important characters in this culture of ours."

2nd Quarter ~ Kids

The next "time out" we should take in our investigation of what's wrong with youth sports deals with the kids themselves. There are some who will say that the kids really have nothing to do with the problems and that all problems must come from adult influences. While many of us would agree that adults are the bigger problem, the kids are not without their faults. Granted, many of those faults stem from the adults in their lives, but they still must be accountable for their actions. So, what are the problems that kids create when it comes to the youth-sports dilemma?

13 ❖ Entitlement

We need to redefine the term athlete. Too many people feel that an athlete is someone with God-given talents and abilities. Kids look up to the boys and girls who have the most natural abilities. They feel that the ones who can run faster, jump higher, or are physically stronger are special. And while they are different because of their natural abilities, they should not be singled out as special. When they are, they too often start to feel a sense of entitlement. Unfortunately, parents, other family members, and coaches often perpetuate this sense. Then a cycle is created because the kids with talent begin to believe in their sense of entitlement. Then other kids buy into this notion and the cycle is, in many ways, complete.

This is too bad. What now happens is that these gifted players start to believe that somehow the rules for everyone else don't apply to them. They may start treating others differently because they believe they are entitled to do so. All this happens because they have some God-given ability that they have had little control over. They were born bigger, faster, or stronger than other kids.

That's not to say that many of these athletes don't work at their games to get bigger, faster, and stronger. Many of them do. But having a genetic advantage does not mean they should be treated as special. Actually, no athlete should be treated in a special way just because he or she is an athlete.

However, when we see a student-athlete who has limited ability but works his or her hardest, has a good attitude, is coachable, is a great teammate, is a good student, and shows great sportsmanship—now that is truly something deserving of praise. We need to talk up those kids more with our youth, so they see the great things that real athletes with character can accomplish. Then, hopefully, they will see that the way to become an athlete who is singled out for his or her accomplishments is to work hard to possess the qualities just mentioned. (For more on "Re-Defining the Term Athlete," check out Bruce Brown's outstanding booklet *Life Lessons for Athletes* at www.proactivecoaching.info.)

It is inevitable that the players with God-given abilities and often a sense of entitlement will continue to grow as players and become the "stars" we see on TV. Now, as players making millions of dollars each year, people are looking to them as role models. Unfortunately, many of them are the worst role models that we could possibly have. They show young kids that: you don't have to practice hard, you can talk back and yell at your coach on the sidelines, you can yell at your teammates if they make mistakes or if they don't make you the focus of everything. You can be rude to women, reporters, and fans, etc. For many people, this is what our professional sports figures have become: leagues of entitled superstars who do whatever they want, whenever they want.

As I sit here writing this, it's almost funny to think that my son acted this same way as a four-year-old. When he didn't get his way, he cried, threw a tantrum, and lashed out at those around him. But he was a little boy, learning that this behavior is wrong. We disciplined him every time he did it, and we still discipline him when he acts inappropriately.

In professional sports, we are talking about grown men and older boys who should have been taught these same lessons—maybe they were taught, but they never learned them, for any number of reasons, from poor home lives, to coaches and parents who didn't instill discipline. And even though they haven't learned discipline yet, we can keep working to instill it. However, as the boy grows into the man, the price is higher because the discipline must now be stronger.

14 ❖ Kids, Now & Then

I hear people go back and forth on the concept that kids are different today than they were years ago. Some people say that kids are no different now, and it's the adults and society that are different. I agree that the adults and society are quite different, and that has had a huge impact on kids. However, I do believe that kids are different now compared to kids of previous generations.

All you have to do is look at pictures of athletes from the last fifty years to see that, physically, there are huge differences between athletes today and athletes back then. The weight room, supplements, training programs, advances in sports medicine and technology all have helped today's athletes become much bigger, faster, and stronger than the athletes of the past, and a lot of this has trickled down to the younger levels. However, physical traits are not the only area where kids have changed.

The biggest areas of difference I see in kids today are in work ethic, innocence, respect, and violence. Now it can be argued that each of these differences stems from either the adults or society in general. But if we say that it's society's fault that kids act the way they do, aren't we just adding to the entitlement problem discussed above? By taking all the accountability for their own behaviors and putting it upon the adults and society in general, don't we just continue to add to the problem and give them an excuse to misbehave?

At some point, though, kids have to look in the mirror and realize that they are in control of their own actions and behaviors. How hard they work or don't work is not Mommy and Daddy's fault. At some point the kids made the decision to do the work or not to do it. The kids made the decision not to work as hard as those who have gone before them and the non-fruits of their non-action will be playing out in their own lives.

As for innocence, respect, and violence, these three seem to go hand-in-hand. I see kids today as having far less innocence than when we Baby Boomers were kids. They are forced to "grow up" so much faster today, and they don't have as much of a chance to just "be a kid." This loss of innocence has also contributed to a lack of respect for so many of the things that, in days gone by, demanded respect, such as for authority, adults, the past, and a myriad of other things.

At the same time, violence among kids has increased at an alarming rate. When we were kids, being in a gang meant you and your friends had a clubhouse or tree fort, with unique rituals that only members of the group would engage in. Now, being in a gang is about vandalism, stealing, fighting, dealing drugs, and even killing rival gang members. Now the stakes are life and death, and more and more kids are playing that game.

So when people say kids are no different today than they used to be, I disagree. I think there are big changes that we need to address in some fashion.

15 ❖ Discipline

Discipline is a funny word. For most people it carries the negative connotation of punishment, but that's not really what the word means. It is meant that way when used as a verb: "I am going to have to discipline you because of your inappropriate behavior." That's how I used the word earlier when talking about having to discipline my son when he was four years old.

When discipline is a noun, or disciplined is used as an adjective, it's not as simple to define. I have read and heard some great definitions through the years. As I mentioned in the section on coaches, Bruce Brown defines discipline as "focused attention and effort," while Bobby Knight says that discipline is "knowing what to do, knowing when to do it, doing it to the best of your abilities, and doing it that way every single time."

I have always liked Coach Knight's definition of discipline, and yet when I look at Bruce Brown's alongside it, I realize that what Coach Knight and Coach Brown are both talking about is focusing one's attention and effort on the task at hand in order to create the desired outcome. And that really is what discipline is all about. When I have discipline, I am doing things or handling myself in the right way. When I don't have discipline, I am doing things or handling myself in the wrong way.

Discipline and Self-Discipline

There are those who say that what Brown and Knight are talking about is self-discipline. I say that self-discipline is the only kind of discipline there is—other than when this word is used to describe punishment. What we're talking about is how one handles oneself. It has nothing to do with others. All right, the exception is when talking about how a team handles itself. Teams must have discipline, too, but ultimately a team is a collection of individuals. If the individuals don't have discipline, the team will be undisciplined. So even there, it still comes down to self-discipline. For those of you stuck on the argument over "discipline" versus "self-discipline," get over it. There is very little difference, if any.

Why is discipline so critical for our kids? Because without it, they will not grow and develop to their full potential. When we teach kids from our perspective as parents, coaches and teachers, we are trying to pass on our experience and expertise to help them grow and develop. We hope they won't make the same mistakes that we did. However, we also know that they must make mistakes along the way in order to grow and develop. We don't expect their lives to be mistake-free; we just want to help them limit their mistakes, so they can enjoy life more and get more out of it.

Consequently, we try to teach our kids what we see as the proper way to behave. From saying "Please" and "Thank you" to raising their hand when asking a question in class to stopping at a stoplight, we are constantly asking kids to become disciplined. The ones who pick it up end up having more success—some take longer than others. The ones who pick up good discipline have either learned the importance of doing things the right way, or it was in their nature to do so. Either way, the disciplined kids generally have more success due to their discipline.

Problems for the Undisciplined

On the other hand, those who are undisciplined seem to go through much more trial and error as they are trying to learn things— with an emphasis on error! Because they lack the discipline to do things the right way and to do them that way every time, they experience more failure. Often they seem to be saying, "I'll show you. My way will work, too!" That can be a good thing, if it is done the right way and not too often, because it is showing perseverance on their part. Unfortunately and too often, undisciplined kids seem to AL-WAYS be trying to show us that their way will work. Also, undisciplined kids often have an attitude that they just don't care to do it the right way or to try what might be a better way. And often they just don't care—period. They don't care about anything but whatever it is they want at that moment.

This need for instant gratification is a huge part of being undisciplined. It takes discipline and "sacrifice" to have success. So many undisciplined kids are not willing to make a sacrifice to have success because it will come at the expense of the moment. To get up and leave the house and their TV or video games or stereo and some junk food to go to school and work out in the weight room for an hour-and-a-half on an afternoon in June, to get ready for football in September, takes far too much discipline than most kids have these days. For kids who play basketball to go out and shoot 500 shots two or three days a week from March to November, to prepare for the season, is just too much to ask of most young people today. Ask Tom Brady or Lebron James how they got to be who they are, and they will tell you what it took in terms of motivation and discipline to get to where they did.

Many high-school kids who play a sport will tell you that they would like to play professionally or get a college scholarship. However, when it comes to doing the things necessary to achieve that goal, they aren't willing to focus their attention and effort enough to do so. This is especially difficult for those kids who have always been bigger, faster, and stronger than their peers. Because of their physical superiority, these kids have not had to work as hard for success, so they often don't have the work ethic necessary to take the next steps. Since they aren't used to having to work so hard to achieve success, when they think about doing the things necessary to get to the next level, they don't think they need to, because they've never had to before.

I know there are many kids who don't have pro or college-sports aspirations. They just want to do their best in high school, get to the state tournament, and win a trophy. While the level of the goal is not as lofty, it is still a huge challenge and one that requires the same level of discipline needed to achieve. In order to have your ultimate success, whatever that may be, you must put in the time necessary to achieve it. Unfortunately, what most kids think is the necessary amount of time, effort, and attention to achieve success, and what really is necessary are two very different things. I am not saying that kids need to be playing their sports 24 hours a day, 7 days a week. In fact, I think they often "play" their sports too much. What they need to do is spend more time "preparing" to play their sports than they do right now. What do I mean by this?

We have an epidemic in youth sports right now. I call it the "AAU mentality." Now, I'm asking the Amateur Athletic Union people (or the people in similar "club" or "elite" types of youth sports organizations) to please hear me out. I have no problem with the concept of your organizations. However, what has happened is that so many kids are now playing some form of organized ball outside of their school settings. They are being bombarded with too much in the way of time commitments, costs, and pressures to win, that they have no time to work at the games they love and time to just be kids. It is all about playing lots of games and winning in these leagues. The emphasis is not enough on practice and developing kids' skills, work ethic, discipline, commitment to their team and to sportsmanship, and too much about winning games.

Watch an AAU game of 4th-grade girls' basketball sometime. For most teams you will see a 2-3 zone defense over 50% of the time. You may see a full-court press from the "good" teams. You will see one "star" player playing a majority of the game and taking a majority of the shots. You will see and hear coaches and parents yelling at their kids, at other kids, and at the officials, much like you will see at high-school games. It is out of control. And I just randomly mentioned 4th-grade girls. I could have picked any age or either gender and the story would be exactly the same. Do we want that for our kids—no matter how old they are?

About halfway through writing this book, my son was nine years old. He had just started playing organized sports in the previous few years. I was excited to be a dad of a kid getting into sports as we embarked on this part of our journey in life. I was also scared to death! I didn't want him to be subjected to what I had seen becoming so commonplace in gyms, baseball fields, football fields, soccer fields, and ice rinks around the country. I wanted him to grow up loving sports the way I did.

Yes, I wanted him to be good at the games he chose to play, but he'd better enjoy them, or else what's the point in playing? I didn't want him telling me at some point down the road that he thinks he'll try another sport because he's tired of how the one he is playing is going. I wanted him to want to try another sport—or musical instrument or whatever—because he had so much fun that he just had to try something else because he wanted to have more of that same kind of fun.

Fortunately, quite a few years later, he is still loving it and he continues to improve at the two sports he plays—basketball and soccer. He realizes that he needs to work at his games to get good at them, but he likes to do that, and he is willing to put in the time to do so. He has not been affected too much by the win-at-all-costs mentality I spoke of above. I'm happy that it hasn't been too out-of-hand. I have seen a variety of people act like idiots at his games, but for the most part, it has been a really good experience for him so far, and we are hoping that continues.

More Practice and Skill Development— Less Playing, Please!

Now you may be thinking, "Okay, Coach, if you're saying that a lot of our kids' sports are out-of-control and too many kids are being made to do way too much, why are you telling us that kids need more discipline to do more things and put in more time to their games?" Because within the framework of their organized sport, what they need more of is teaching how to do it and a little less of actually doing it. Let me explain.

At the high school in our community where I coached for 5 of the last 8 years, our basketball teams play eighteen regular season games, plus a guarantee of at least two post-season games. In order to get through those 20 games, they end up practicing about fifty times throughout the season, with an average practice time of about two hours. That is a ratio of about 2.5:1 practices to games. It's good, but it could be better. A ratio of 3:1 would really allow teams the chance to develop the elements necessary for kids to succeed. Unfortunately, they don't have the time to do that in the season—and basketball is a long season.

In the youth leagues, however, it's usually the exact opposite. They often play more games than they have practices, or at least it evens out to about a 1:1 ratio of practices to games. Their practices are usually about an hour to an hour-and-a-half long. What can you do in an hour with kids of any age, let alone with kids who have limited-to-no experience playing the game? Not much. Then we throw them out on the court into games, we yell at them and their teammates, we yell at their officials. How warped is it that we then expect them to have success and enjoy it? As they get older, the ones who have played more on their own usually stay with it because they are experiencing some success; the others have often gotten sick of it and quit.

So now these elite kids go around their area and around their state and even around the country playing in tournaments with little in the way of practice in skill development. In basketball, for instance, most of their practices are a few shooting drills and fast-break drills, and then scrimmage time where coaches teach set plays and zone defenses. It's all about playing games, strategy, and running plays, even in practice.

Now when these kids get into high school, they believe that their sport should be about playing games, not practicing at the game. The skills that these athletes have are not nearly what they should be. Given the game experience that they have, to now ask them to practice the fundamentals of the game on their own for an hour a day in the off-season and a couple of hours a day during the season would require way more effort, discipline, and sacrifice on their part than they are used to giving. Since this has not been the expectation before, it's going to be hard to get it to become an expectation now—especially since it's much more fun to just play the games!

So here is the double-edged sword or the great paradox—we want our kids to grow up and have fun at their games, but we want them to develop the skills, discipline, sportsmanship, and commitment to team necessary to be good athletes. How do we/they do this? We need to let kids play their games, but we also need to teach them how to play. We need to give them the structure and the discipline to learn how to be part of a sport, but we also have to provide them a venue in which to play that sport without pressure to win and to always be the best.

Why do we need a scoreboard for kids playing sports in first, second, and third grade? Who cares who wins the game? Some of the kids do, but most of them don't, so why should we? Unfortunately, too many adults focus on this aspect, too. In the valley in Washington where I used to live, a friend of mine was refereeing a third-grade boys' AAU game. The coach of one of the teams was getting a bit out of hand, and my friend had to tell him to settle down and calm his behavior. After the game, the coach half-heartedly apologized, and said that they were going for their 82nd win in a row, and so he was way into it.

My friend (who is a varsity basketball coach) was stunned. Here is a team of third-graders who have won 82 games in a row! While that might seem like a great accomplishment, there's a much bigger issue here. When my son was in third grade, he had probably played 30–40 organized games of basketball in his short life. I wasn't keeping track. This coach's team of kids the same age had won more than double the amount of games than my son had actually played. Who knows how many games they played before the 82-game winning streak? The other problem here is that the coach was keeping track! My gosh, they're 8–9 years old! Who cares how many games they have won? And if you are placing so much emphasis on winning, what is that doing to the kids on the team?

Kids at younger ages (kindergarten to 4th grade) don't need adults placing so much emphasis on winning. As they get older, introduce the concept of winning and losing, not as the be-all and end-all of the games, but only as a part of it. Kids will put their own emphasis on winning and losing without our help as they get older. Early on, they don't need it.

We had a program in our school in Washington called Little Dribblers. It was for third-to-sixth graders. Once a week for six weeks in the fall and spring, the kids came into the gym for an hour-and-a-half. They worked on fundamentals for an hour and then they played games for half an hour—they loved it! They learned how to play and then turned around and played. There was no scoreboard; they were just playing for the love of playing. Then four times during those six weeks, we had other teams from other schools in our area come in on a Saturday and play some games. For those days, we did have a scoreboard, but if we had any problems with parents or fans yelling or complaining about it, we turned the scoreboard off. It was awesome.

Youth sports should be about teaching kids how to play. You teach them what's important and hopefully teaching the adults the same thing. I would love to eventually create entire leagues devoted to doing it the right way.

16 ❖ Kids Are Impressionable

It is important for us to remember that kids of all ages are extremely impressionable. Because of this, we adults must always be aware of what we are saying and doing. And it's especially about what we're doing, because so often what we say and how we act are two different things. Kids pick up on that.

Think back to when you were a kid. What do you remember about your teachers, coaches, and other adults who had an impression on you? Chances are, you are remembering what they did, not what they said. Now, that doesn't mean that we don't need to pay attention to our words, which also have power and a huge impact on kids. In fact, chances are that one of the reasons you remember the actions of that adult is that he or she said something that had great impact on you, often right at the time of the action you are remembering. Let me give you an example.

I remember a few of my high-school teachers' classes quite well. My senior year English teacher, Mr. Silkowski, was a great teacher. He was not a coach, not a jock, and probably didn't even like sports much—but our class had a lot of athletes in it, and to put it nicely, not many of them were headed to becoming rocket-science majors in college. In fact, not many of them were even heading to college. Now as I look back at that class with the experience of being a teacher for eighteen years, I think that would have been an incredibly difficult class to teach. And yet, I remember my jock friends really liking that class and liking Mr. Silkowski, even though the class was fairly difficult, and he did not come off as an athletic kind of guy. What he was, though, was an entertaining, witty teacher, who held our attention, who demanded that we be attentive and disciplined, and who kept us interested in the subject matter.

I remember those things because of the way Mr. Silkowski acted much more than the words that he said. However, I do remember one thing he said—well actually, it was the same thing he said on a variety of occasions. When the class would act up and not respond properly after a few of his entreaties for us to settle down, he would close the book he was reading from or discussing, stop talking, fold his arms, and in a matter-of-fact tone say, "Not happy." That was it. We knew it was time to stop.

Now it's interesting that 40 years later, I don't remember what, if anything, ever happened after that. In fact, I don't believe anything ever did. We respected Mr. Silkowski so much that we knew it was time to shut up and pay attention. We didn't want to upset him anymore because: 1) we didn't want to find out the consequences, and 2) more importantly, we didn't want him to be mad at us because we didn't want to let him down.

So as you can see, while what Mr. Silkowski said was certainly important in this situation, it was his actions that made what he said carry so much weight. This is what I mean by how important it is for us as coaches and teachers to be aware of both our actions and our words. Kids latch on to things that we say and do all the time, and often we don't even know it.

We May Never Know the Power of Our Words

This point was nailed home to me about twenty years ago when I was out having dinner with a couple of teacher-friends. An ex-student of ours came up to my best friend, Bob, whom I had grown up with since the age of five. Bob went to a different college than I, and then we ended up teaching and coaching at the same high school for eleven years. This student stopped by our table to say, "Hi." We exchanged not more than a minute of small talk when all of a sudden the kid said to Bob, "I just want you to know that I've really turned things around. I'm about to graduate from college with a degree in Business Administration and have a couple of job offers. I'm trying to decide which one to take."

Bob said, "Wow, Sean, that's great. Congratulations."

Sean said, "Well, I wanted to tell you that, 'cause do you remember when I was a freshman, and we were reading . . ." and he named whatever book they were reading in class at the time. And Bob said that he remembered because he always taught that book to his freshmen. Sean then went on to tell Bob something like, "Remember when you said . . ." and it was some statement that Bob was able to work into the lesson from the story. In Bob's mind, it wasn't that big of a deal, but to Sean it was. Then Sean said, "I never forgot that. I didn't really know if I wanted to go to college, but when you said that, I knew I had to. Once I was in college, whenever I was struggling and thinking I didn't want to keep going on, I always thought about when you said that, and that got me re-focused on finishing the class and finishing my degree. Thanks a lot, Mr. K. I don't think I could have done it without you."

Now, anyone who has been a teacher for any length of time has his or her own stories of kids who have told them what an impact that teacher had on him or her. It is because of these moments why many of us teach. (It certainly isn't the money!) But that's not the most important point of the story. Here's the kicker.

Sean shook our hands, said good-bye, turned and walked away. As he walked away, Bob turned toward me and said, "I have no idea what he's talking about. I don't ever remember saying that."

That hit me hard. Here was a kid who just told us that my friend's words were as large a catalyst as anything in the kid's life for making him turn from failure to success, and my friend couldn't re-member what he said. I said to Bob, "My God, think about all the throw away lines we have ever stood in front of a class and said to kids. Imagine how many times a kid was sitting out there, and one of those lines was actually hitting that kid straight to the heart." That moment taught me how important it is that we always say and do the right things all the time in front of kids. I have passed that story on to many of my teacher and coach colleagues because I hope that they, too, will remember that their words and actions can have such a huge impact on a child.

17 ❖ What's Cool & Not Cool

Kids have always worried about what their friends and peers think about them. They are very concerned with what is considered "cool" or "lame," to use words that have been popular in the last couple of decades. (Even using "cool" and "lame" may not be cool anymore. Seventy-five years ago you only heard those two words used when talking about temperature and horses!)

It is all about feeling accepted. If kids feel accepted wherever they are, then everything is "cool." But if they don't feel accepted, look out. The radar for "lame" comes up, and they will do everything in their power to figure out how to get back to that level of acceptance where they feel that everything is okay the way it is.

"Cool" in the Sports World

Unfortunately, we in the sports world fight this everyday. If athletes think that doing something to improve themselves is not "cool," we struggle to get them to do it. From wearing certain styles of uniforms or practice gear, to doing certain drills and techniques to improving their game, if kids think it diminishes their level of "cool," a coach or parent will be hard-pressed to get them to do it. However, the moment something comes along that is deemed "cool" (or "dope" in the vernacular of 2018), kids are all over it.

In the eighties and nineties, the use of steroids and other supplements was just starting to be a huge issue in professional sports. Actually, it had been an issue for years, but it became a big media issue as more stories of athletes using them to improve performance hit the papers. We coaches had to start addressing supplement use with our kids. For a while in the nineties, creatine was the big thing. I know athletes use it still, and it is considered a supplement that is good for building muscle, but I don't hear nearly as much about it anymore.

As for steroids, they have received such negative publicity in the media through the last two decades, with high-profile athletes falling from grace, that I think kids are seeing them as "uncool" nowadays, much more than before. If so, that's a good thing.

However, too often kids see and hear about things that professional athletes or others are doing that they think are cool, when what they are doing is anything but cool. Of course, alcohol, drug, tobacco, and e-cigarette use are certainly some of the biggest issues to deal with here. Kids think it is cool to party like adults. They see or read about their sports, music, or movie heroes out at the clubs drinking or doing drugs and think it's the thing to do. I know that all kids get the urge to experiment with adult types of things at some point. However, the younger the age at which this is happening and its frequency is becoming scary.

What else has become "cool"? Tattoos—they've been the in-thing for some time now. It seems like every major professional athlete has a tattoo of some sort. I don't have a problem with tattoos. However, what has happened is that kids now think that they need a tattoo to be "cool." Piercings have also become cool. Most kids nowadays have at least their ears pierced, but many more are getting noses, navels, lips, tongues, eyebrows, and a few other unmentionables pierced. It is alarming to me to consider how many of our kids are doing these things.

There are certainly other things that kids find cool nowadays that may not have been considered cool before (or didn't even exist before). And if you are reading this in the future from when it was published, there are probably even newer things that kids think are cool that we will in some way need to deal with. No matter what the new cool thing is, remember that what's cool and not cool drive so many of our young people to act the way they do.

Rise Above What's Cool & Do What's Right

So what does all this have to do with youth sports? In order to get kids to develop and succeed at their sports, they sometimes have to do things that their peers may view as "uncool." Sometimes we will demand that they do things that they perceive as "lame." If we truly believe that what we are asking them to do is instrumental to their success, and it is not totally embarrassing to them, then we must stick to our guns and demand that it be done. If we are doing something strictly to humiliate them, we certainly need to rethink it. On the other hand, just because kids say something is lame and they won't do it doesn't mean we should give it up. Again, if it has value and you believe it is important to their success, demand it. Those who want to be a part of it will do what it takes. Those who don't will weed themselves out. Let me give an example.

Kids today hate wearing the short shorts that we wore to play basketball back in the seventies. The style now is long and baggy. I used to intentionally purchase shorts that were not long and baggy to prove a point that it's not the clothes that make the difference; it's how you play. However, as time went by, and longer shorts became the norm, I acquiesced. I realized that my kids were feeling truly embarrassed at how they looked out there. That was never my goal. I just wanted them to not worry so much about how they looked and worry more about how they played. As long as they gave great effort, were committed to each other, and handled themselves with class and character, I didn't care if our shorts were longer than before.

Also, they all had to wear the same color shoes, all white socks below the calf, and wristbands only if I okayed them. It was not that I wanted to be a dictator with all kinds of power. It was that I wanted us to be a team, not a group of individuals. Also, I think it is good for kids to have to occasionally do some things that they don't want to do. I don't know if that was my parents' goal, but they instilled that concept in me when I was a kid, and I saw it help me to be a better adult. I found that there are things that I didn't want to do as an adult and came to realize they had to be done, so I'd just better do them and not whine about it. As a kid, I whined about it, if not out loud to my parents, then to myself. But that helped teach me the value of working at things that needed to be done, whether I wanted to or not. So I often had kids do some things that they didn't want to do.

Finally, I sometimes would have kids do things that might seem uncool at the time, but I felt would help us bond as a team better or help the individual become a better player. I have long felt that one thing that holds kids back is this concern that, "If I don't look cool doing this thing, I'm not going to do it." The classic one that comes to mind is when a kid dribbles a ball off his foot after trying to do some difficult move with the ball. You will often see that kid try to nonchalantly go back to get the ball as if to "maintain some cool" even though he just did something that looked "uncool." The outcome, more often than not, is that an opponent, who cares nothing about how cool he is or who feels that the coolest thing is to beat his opponent, will race to pick up the ball and fling it to a teammate for a basket at the other end.

Now we have a kid with a fragile ego because, while he lost the ball, he is also concerned that he has lost his cool persona. Now he is determined to show people that either: 1) he still is very cool, or 2) he will make up for that little mistake that rarely happens to him, or 3) he will not play hard, because if he does, he might fail, and to fail when trying your hardest is totally uncool, or 4) he may now be scared to handle the ball. All of these scenarios are not good for our team, because we now have an individual thinking only of himself and not of how his team needs him.

Better to Look Cool Rather than Giving Your Best

The third scenario above is the one that I most want to address. I see this so often in athletics at the middle-school and high-school levels these days. Kids are so concerned with how they look or how they are being perceived, that they will not put forth maximum effort. I see two reasons for this.

First, if a kid puts forth maximum effort, he might feel that he doesn't look cool. He doesn't have that swagger, that strut that says, "I am in total control even though I look like I am just walking around." So instead of working as hard as he possibly can, he cruises. "No matter that I am not performing at my best; at least I look cool doing it." The irony, of course, is that the person beating you looks that much cooler because he is outperforming you.

In fact, kids nowadays have a name that they call someone who doesn't have the kind of cool described above. They call him a "Try-Hard." Understand that being called a try-hard is not a compliment. To me that is as big a problem as there is. Since when did trying hard become an uncool thing? And often, those calling others "try-hards" are the better players and leaders. What a shame! Those should be the very players modeling what it truly means to be one who tries hard. But because they are perceived as "cool" by others, and they are saying that trying hard is not cool, it just gives those who want to give great effort and be their best for the team a bad rap, and makes it tougher on those players and the entire team to become the best that they can be.

Fear of Failure When Giving Your Best

The second reason for kids to not put forth maximum effort is that if one puts forth maximum effort, he is taking a huge risk, and he becomes extremely vulnerable. How so? Because if he gives it everything he's got and fails, he might be perceived as a loser. However, if he doesn't give it his all and he loses, he can always say, "Well, I wasn't trying very hard anyway. If I would have tried harder, I would have won."

That is a very scary, and yet very common occurrence with youth sports today. In fact, I believe it is on the rise, because there is so much pressure to win nowadays that kids just crack and decide not to give it their all, so they don't have to worry about the pressure to perform their best. "If I don't give it my best, I can't fail, because I wasn't really trying. That way if we lose or I don't get the scholarship that my parents want me to get, it's not really my fault. So there really is no pressure after all."

I remember one player in my years as a basketball coach who took this to an extreme. She was projected to be a very good player coming out of eighth grade. She was good enough to play a lot of varsity minutes right from the start of her freshman year. But her parents and everyone else who knew her had such high expectations for her that she quickly started to plateau when things got tougher.

She had been a scorer in eighth grade. But in high school, she did not do much in the way of scoring, at least not consistently. When you watched her play in games, it looked like she was having no fun. She was so worried about making a mistake that she made a lot of mistakes, and she didn't take risks. However, the biggest area where she made it clear to me that she had a major fear of failure was in practice one year.

She was one of the better players on the team. We had nine total players on the varsity, so I had to scrimmage with them. I always matched up against her because she was the biggest kid on the team. Time and time again, she refused to take shots when she was wide open, even though she was one of the best players on the team. When her teammates would tell her to shoot the ball, she would yell back at them that she didn't want to, that she wouldn't make it anyway.

The moment the competition got too tough (me), she went into a shell. She couldn't handle the fact that she might fail—and this was at practice! When we would shoot free throws together, I would turn it into a little contest. Whoever makes more wins the game. The moment she got down a little bit, she would go into a shell, and not even try to make her free throws. It was easier for her to give up than to compete.

Interestingly enough, each of the last two years she was just good enough to make the Honorable Mention All-Conference team. Both times she found out that she had made that team, she was disappointed because she wanted to be first or second team. But she hadn't done what needed to be done to make those teams. She refused to put in the effort, and more importantly the risk, necessary to have that kind of success and the accompanying reward that would come with it. Fortunately, she turned things around a bit in her senior year under a new coach, and she began to compete more fearlessly. She ended up as a Second Team All-Conference player when she finally shed her fear of failure and played as hard as she could.

This player's situation is not at all unique. I would imagine that every team in the nation has at least one kid like this. We all deal with players who are extremely concerned with how they are perceived, especially when it comes to the acceptance of what is cool or not. We must try to instill in these players at a young age that what is cool is going out and giving everything you've got to achieve success. We also need to show them that what is cool is giving yourself over completely to your teammates in such a way that you are willing to go through all kinds of things with them. Finally, we must show kids that handling oneself with class and character and being a good sport are the ultimate in cool. If you want to distinguish yourself and get noticed, you do so by being the classiest players and team that anyone has ever seen.

I have spent years hammering this point home to high-school boys and girls, and I have been very pleased and very proud of the results. I can't tell you how many times I have had people comment to me on how well-mannered, well-behaved, polite, and classy our kids have been. Those are the moments that mean the most to me. Oh sure, I like winning championships like anyone else. But when I have teams that win sportsmanship awards or receive accolades and praise for their behavior, it means so much more to me, because it is something the players have total control over, whereas there are many other factors that contribute to winning or losing games. They have also learned behaviors that will carry them into successful adult lives.

Players are often looked at as an extension and a reflection of their coaches. I don't care all that much if that extension produces a win, but I care deeply if that reflection shows a good person who treats others with respect. There is no greater tribute to the job that I have. I am so grateful to all of the kids who I have coached over the years who have helped to foster this concept of our teams.

18 ❖ Language & Inappropriate Behaviors

On the heels of talking about character, class, and sportsmanship, let's look at some of the things that tear those elements apart. These are things that we coaches and adults must address if we are to mend the fabric of youth sports that is being torn up. The first element is language. I am amazed at how bad the language of our kids has gotten in the last twenty years. Now I know that kids have sworn and used bad language forever. I understand that. However, nowadays it is so much more prevalent than ever before.

There are many reasons for this breakdown. Society is probably the biggest culprit. We hear so many bad words on television and in movies and music today that kids are bombarded with it. Those same words are coming out of kids' parents' mouths because they grew up with those words, too. However, when parents were growing up, kids said them only with each other, and they only heard them from the occasional gutter mouth adult and the few R-rated movies that they might sneak in to see. Now, with every home having cable or satellite TV, and streaming movies on their laptops, tablets, and phones, or playing M-rated video games (Mature, for ages 17 and up) on a nightly basis, it's no wonder that kids are being bombarded by bad language. Also, listen to your kids' playlist of his or her favorite musical artists and chances are you'll be F-bombed into oblivion.

I remember when I was in junior high school and the song "Sunshine" by Jonathan Edwards was popular on the radio. I remember driving in the car with my dad and that song being on and him hearing the line, "He can't even run his own life. I'll be damned if he'll run mine." Oh, my God! I thought my dad was going to have a heart attack. That radio was turned off so fast, you'd have thought that it was a nuclear device that had just been armed for attack. Then he proceeded to yell at me about it, as if I had anything to do with what songs they played on the radio. After that whenever I heard that song coming on the radio with either my mom or dad around, I quickly turned it to another station.

I laugh when I think back to that time because now it seems so innocent. However, it was the start of the problem. As our standards and mores relaxed in the seventies, we started to set the tone for what is going on today. People must not have realized that by opening the doors on censorship and behaviors, we would ultimately release a flood of inappropriateness that is now consuming our society and having huge ramifications on kids. Don't get me wrong; I am against censorship. I believe that people have the right to say and do what they want within the law and without inciting hate or harm upon others. However, I think that we have gone too far in what we allow on TV, movies, and music.

I personally have no problem with bad language and other "adult" behavior for adults. When I watch a mob or action movie, a well-placed F-word has no equal. When I see scantily clad women in movies with a sexual content, I'm okay with it. But I am a fifty-plus-year-old adult male. I can pick and choose what movies I watch and what language I hear. But when my kids were bombarded with all kinds of images and language like this in movies designated as PG or PG-13 as they were growing up, I had and still have a problem with that.

Yes, I know PG stands for Parental Guidance, and we should guide what our kids see. But we don't always get the chance to do that at the movies they may go to with friends, or on the phone, tablet, or computer that they have access to everywhere now. And when it says PG-13, the assumption is that it is something appropriate for kids 13 years old and up. Have you seen the comedy movies designated as PG-13? Many of them are hilarious—but appropriate for 13-year-olds? Hardly.

And keep in mind that many kids quite a bit younger than 13 are seeing these movies, too. Turn on any show on the main TV networks now, and you are dealing with much of the same stuff. And don't get me started talking about cable or satellite TV! So don't tell me that it is my job as a parent to guide what they're exposed to. Of course, that is my job, but it is also our job as members of a society to help in the guiding.

I was a high school English teacher for eighteen years. In my classes of seniors who were 17 and 18, should I have been using the standard of what's acceptable in an R-rated movie to determine the material in my literature class? I should think not. As a teacher and influential member of society, I had an obligation to help with that guidance usually delegated to parents. So do you. So does everyone. Parental guidance needs to extend beyond parents. So with regard to language and inappropriateness, we all need to take some responsibility and teach our kids (mostly by example) the proper way to act in this society.

Deal with It

Teachers and coaches play a role in this, too. While we don't set the tone for parental guidance of every kid, we sure can help deal with it by doing just that—deal with it! When I hear a kid use foul language or say inappropriate things, I address it. Yes, I know that kids swear and say bad words. That doesn't mean I have to accept it as okay when it happens. They need to know what is acceptable and unacceptable in a civil society. While I may not be the be-all and end-all of civility, I can at least get them thinking about what they are saying.

Also, as a teacher/coach, I must watch my own words and behaviors. Just like I know kids hear bad language and see inappropriate behaviors on a regular basis, I don't have to be one of the people using it in front of them (or worse yet, towards them). Kids take their cues as to what is acceptable and unacceptable from adults. While their own parents' behavior may not always be the best, we teachers and coaches should make sure that we are not feeding into the notion that bad language is acceptable for kids to use in these kinds of public and team settings.

There are other behaviors that kids do that fall into the category of inappropriate that we adults need to work together to eliminate. Obviously, any illegal activities are things that we must not allow. The use of alcohol, drugs, and tobacco are all elements that we cannot tolerate from our kids. These are the obvious ones. But there are other behaviors that we cannot tolerate as well. Acting up in class, causing problems in the halls at school, hazing, and any types of bullying and harassment are all problems that we in the athletic world need to address with our teams. There are some people who would say that those things are not part of the team, so it is not our problem. However, it is part of the team because these behaviors affect the team, and they affect others' perceptions of the team.

Take hazing for example. If we have kids hazing other kids and I don't know about it, there could be some very serious issues happening that I have no clue about. While many teams have mild initiation rites and ceremonies, these are the stepping-stones to much bigger situations that can eventually lead to headline-grabbing news, even tragedy. But even on the smallest scale, hazing and initiations can create team problems by causing divisions and bitterness amongst teammates. Most kids think it's just a rite of passage, but there are many kids who are very private, sensitive people, and their self-esteem or confidence can be shattered by what someone else might consider to be no big deal. We as coaches need to teach our teams that there is no place for behaviors such as hazing, and we must be cognizant of team chemistry and relationships. While we can't be there at all times and we won't ever know all that happens with our teams, we must at least work to stay in touch with them, so that we can be there if things start to go in a direction we don't want.

While kids will be kids, we must help kids understand what is appropriate and what is not when it comes to being an athlete. This must start at a very young age, so that when they get older, it is already expected of them. Start instilling proper behaviors in teams for all kids at all ages right from the start of their experience. This is not only beneficial for the young people, but it will also make it easier for all of these kids' future coaches and teachers. Kids expect that the way they are taught and coached is the way it is done everywhere else, especially at a young age, so it behooves every coach to instill those same elements of good behavior.

This is a strong reason why we need to start mandating that coaches of youth leagues all around the nation be trained in coaching effectiveness. Otherwise, we run the risk of our kids' poor behaviors being allowed, and in some instances even fostered, by coaches who have no clue what constitutes good coaching. Just watch a few episodes of *Friday Night Tykes*, the Netflix docuseries that dives into the cutthroat world of Texas youth football. You will see some of these coaches allowing and fostering the wrong types of behaviors, from using bad language to telling kids to go out and hurt the other team's members. There is no place for these kinds of people leading our young people. However, if we have coaches who have a good understanding of what to be instilling in their kids, youth sports and school sports will be far better off because kids will have a better understanding of the proper way to be an athlete.

3rd Quarter ~
Parents

And now the section you've all been waiting for—PARENTS! While that is meant somewhat tongue-in-cheek, this is the section where many people believe we will get at the root of all of the problems associated with youth sports. Amazingly enough, even though I am a coach, I disagree. Don't get me wrong. I think parents are a huge issue—maybe the biggest one—but they are not the only cause, nor are they the root of the problem, other than the fact that they bring the children into the world around whom these problems revolve. Many kid problems are due to poor parenting issues, but still, parents are the ones more than any other who have the biggest stake in this and the biggest chance to make things better, so in many ways, they are also going to be the biggest part of the solution.

I'm sure that many parents will get on the defensive with many of the statements I'll make in this section. My response to them would be, "Why are you being so defensive?" Most of the time, people get on the defensive because someone has hit a nerve and touched upon something that rings true. So, if you're a parent, please try to remain open to all that is brought up here. For the first chapters of this book, I had to do the same thing for coaches as I explored the shortcomings of people in my profession, myself included. It is ALWAYS a good thing to examine yourself in this way, because it helps you see yourself a little more clearly, often by observing how the rest of the world sees you. Also, I'm sure that some parents will be saying things like, "Well, of course he sees it that way. He's a coach." Two points about that:

1) While I am a coach, I am also a parent. I am step-father to a 28-year-old woman who played sports in school and a father to a 17-year-old boy who plays sports now. I, too, have had to deal with some of the things that other parents deal with.

2) You wouldn't believe how many parents, some who have coached and some who haven't, have said to me, "I could never coach. The parents would drive me nuts. I'd kill one of them!" Ironically, the parents who have said this have often been parents who are some of the worst. Usually though, it is parents who see things quite clearly as to what we coaches have to deal with, and who realize that it's not easy being a coach, that is, a surrogate dad/mom, coun-selor, and friend to THEIR children. So, while you will get my perspective as a coach, it's the same perspective of many parents who have never coached a day in their lives.

19 ❖ The Situations/Problems

So, what are the problems with parents? Well, there are many. In no particular order, here are the ones that I see as the biggest:

- Living vicariously through their kids

- Not caring about their kids' sports

- Unrealistic view of their kids' abilities

- Unrealistic expectations of their kids playing at the next level

- Focused more on their own goals for their kids' involvement in sports rather than their kids' goals

- Too much emphasis on winning

- Too much emphasis on their kids' playing time

- Too much emphasis on their kids' sports instead of academics

- Belief that they know more than the coaches, referees, or umpires

- Sticking up for their kids even when their kids have done something wrong

- Over-analyzing their kids' own play

- Giving their kids a sense of entitlement

- Generally feeling that they know more than everyone else

It's kind of funny, but when you watch or listen to parents, they often will say things to make you believe that they feel they have the parenting thing all figured out and anyone who does it differently is all screwed up. All of us do this to some degree. Obviously, we feel that at any given time, the course of action we are taking is the right one; otherwise, we wouldn't be taking it. But it is interesting to see how far parents take this behavior when it comes to their own kids in sports.

I know I don't have all the answers on parenting, but there are times when I think that I do. I often use my experiences growing up to determine how my kids should be behaving. Sometimes that's fine. When my parents instilled in me that you say *please* and *thank you* to people, that was a good thing, and I have tried to do the same with my kids. But there are other things that my parents did while raising me that might not be the best course of action for me to take when raising mine today. Times have changed, so I have to keep in mind that there are many alternatives when choosing courses of action in raising kids.

Coaching has its similarities to parents raising kids, and it has its differences. Kids need all their adult role models to provide guidance, discipline, love, respect, etc. The difference for coaches comes into play when you realize that building a team is different than building a family. You constantly hear coaches talk about how their team is a family. That can be good. Just remember, though, that families can be dysfunctional. Good families have much of the same qualities that good teams have, and vice versa, but it's interesting to note that great parents don't always make great coaches. Likewise, we often see great coaches struggle to be great parents to their own kids. We also see some coaches who are parents themselves struggle to treat other coaches the right way. Both of these situations occur because there are differences in the dynamics of parenting and coaching. Let's get down to specifics.

20 ❖ Playing Time

As I discussed earlier, playing time is the issue that parents want to talk with coaches about more than any other. In my 30+ years of coaching, I can remember only a couple of parent meetings where the parents came in to discuss my strategy and how I ran the program. Other than that, every parent meeting centered around one thing—playing time. I was fortunate that I didn't have too many parent complaints, but the ones I did have were often not pleasant. It's a shame, but so often the coach/parent relationship ends up being an adversarial one. Ironically, we both want their kid to have a good experience; however, we sometimes have different ideas about what that means.

Coaches need to understand that there is nothing wrong with parents wanting more playing time for their kids, but it's how parents deal with the situation that is usually the problem. Many parents are fine with the amount of playing time their kids get. Obviously, the ones who play a lot are okay with it. But others whose kids don't play so much are okay with it, too, if they are realistic enough to understand that their child is not at the same ability level as the others who are playing more.

Please refer to the *Playing Time* chapter for coaches in this book (Chapter 10), for the specifics of how a coach should handle playing-time concerns and issues. Also, I have written the bookl, *Playing Time: Guidelines for Coaches, Athletes, and Parents*, in which I discuss in much greater detail some ideas on this issue and how best to deal with it. (See the Bibliography at the end of this book.)

Player/Coach Meeting

So what can parents do about their child's playing time or about having a child be cut from the team? Well, the first thing parents should do is ask their child if he talked to the coach. Talking to the coach should always be the first step in the process for kids in the middle-school ages and older. For younger ages, it is good for them to try to start that conversation, too. However, parents may want to get involved early on with younger players.

Find out what the coach told him. If he didn't talk to the coach, the parent can tell the child that he must talk to the coach. Sometimes kids are hesitant to talk to the coach. It is up to the parent to help the child in this instance. Offer some ideas as to how to open the conversation and what kinds of things to ask, such as in the examples that follow. The child should be respectful at all times and find out why he didn't make the team or why he isn't playing much. If this is done in a respectful manner, the coach should have no problem with sitting down and talking to the child. Saying something like, "Excuse me, Coach. Can I talk to you in private for a moment?" is a great start.

Then, when in private, a statement like, "Coach, I don't understand why I don't play very much," or "Coach, what do I need to do to get more playing time?" is a good beginning. Tell your child to look the coach in the eye as he asks the question, and then listen intently to the answer. He should continue to ask questions if he needs clarification on anything he doesn't understand. If your child disagrees with things the coach says, he can voice the disagreement, as long as it is done in a respectful manner. Ending the discussion with a "Thanks for letting me come in and talk, Coach," or something like that, is another way to show the coach respect.

Compare that situation to what many athletes actually do. Many times, rather than respectfully going in and speaking to their coach, they will pout. They will avoid eye contact with the coach at practice. They will not work hard in practice. They often are making comments in the back of lines in drills. When they are addressed about their behavior, they roll their eyes and act like either they know nothing about what the coach is saying, or they can't believe the coach would say such a thing to them.

I have never understood how a kid could believe that I would be thinking to myself, "Wow, Jimmy is pouting, sulking and not working hard at all. He's not paying attention when I'm speaking, and he's rolling his eyes at me every time I call him out. I think he needs to be rewarded with more playing time!" In all my years of coaching, I've always tried to find some playing time for the kid who came in and respectfully talked to me about it, because he did what was asked of him and handled himself in the way we taught our kids to do.

The Logistics of the Parent Meeting with the Coach

If the child did talk to the coach and the parent is still not satisfied, the parent can then set up a time to talk. Again, this needs to be done in a respectful manner. The first rule is to never approach the coach with your concerns before, during, or after a game. We usually extend this boundary to include practices as well, but for some coaches, the time after practice actually works well. The best way to handle this, though, is to call ahead and set up an appointment at a time that works well for both coach and parents.

When they finally do meet, the parent should politely ask why the child was cut or not playing much. The parent needs to allow the coach the chance to speak without feeling like s/he is being attacked. If the parent wants to know specific things that his child could have done or needs to do in the future, that is perfectly acceptable to ask. Both the coach and the parents need to maintain their composure. This can sometimes be difficult, as emotions can be running a bit high in these meetings.

A problem can arise when parents want to start talking about other kids, and this happens often in these kinds of meetings. Immediately, these parents want to compare their daughter to some other girl on the team who they think is not as good as their daughter. Parents should avoid doing this. They are meeting with the coach to talk about their child, not someone else's.

As a coach, I always tried to nip this in the bud unless it was the best way to help explain why the daughter didn't make the team or didn't play as much as she would like to. Usually, I would say, "Wait a minute. We are here to talk about your daughter, not Suzie Jones. I will be happy to tell you about your daughter's play and her week in tryouts, but I am not about to start bringing other kids into the discussion. Let's focus on your daughter, since that is why you came in to meet with me." Usually, this was all it took to re-direct the discussion back to their daughter. If parents understand this going into the meeting, it helps things go a little smoother.

What most parents can expect to hear from a coach in one of these meetings is an explanation of how the coach views the kid's abilities. No matter the sport, if she has been cut or is not playing much, there are skill deficiencies that she has, unless she has a poor attitude and that is the only thing keeping her from playing. But honestly, while we talk about attitude being the most important thing, if a kid has great skills and a poor attitude, most coaches aren't going to cut her. The coach will take a chance that he can help her with her attitude because he knows that since she has some skills, she could help the program out. Coaches are often willing to roll the dice on that player. However, if a player has lesser skills and the coach sees no chance of her ever getting playing time because of her ability level, he will often cut that player. While it may seem harsh, it is the reality, especially of high school varsity competition. At some point, the kid has to have the skills that allow her to play at that level.

The biggest dilemma with regards to this situation is when you have a kid who has very little talent but is a great kid who does everything that is asked of him, works incredibly hard, is all about team, is a good student, and never misses a workout all year long. You hate to cut this kid more than anyone else. Early in my career, I didn't cut this kind of kid, and it came back and bit me at times. This "great-attitude" kid started being a problem as the season went on because he wasn't playing much at all. After a few years of that happening, I decided it is better to cut that kid loose. I hated that because I was cutting kids who I knew were good role models for behavior in our program, but I was concerned they would turn out like the other kids who became problems.

A couple years later, I settled on the strategy that I would sit the kid down and let him tell me what he wanted to do. I basically offered three options:

1) "I will cut you, and you can blame me."
(Not necessarily that blunt, but that message)

2) "You can be on the team, but you must understand that you will not play except in rare cases. You must handle this with a good attitude. If you become a problem, I will have to let you go at that time."

3) "You can swing; that is, you will play some quarters on the JV and some on the varsity. The number of quarters you play on each will depend on the game."

None of these options is ideal or perfect in any way, but it at least gives kids a chance to determine what they would like to see happen with regards to their athletic experience. Usually, the kid will take one of the last two options, sometimes in combination. They often start out just on varsity and then realize that they miss playing, so they come and ask me if they can swing. Sometimes they do just the opposite. Either way, they feel they have some say in the matter, which helps them keep their self-respect and move forward.

Also, by offering the player these options, I think I have dealt with fewer parents. When the parents ask the kid why he is doing whichever option he chooses, the kid can tell them that he chose to do it that way. I believe this makes the parent have a little less incentive to come in and make it an issue with me, since his kid has chosen his own path.

Without question, a good side effect of doing it this way is that I don't have to be the ultimate bad guy who cut the kid. I am a human being. I have feelings and emotions, too. As I have said before, there is little that is worse for us as coaches than cutting a kid. Although I don't like the actual experience, I don't mind cutting kids who I know won't help the program or, more importantly, have done nothing to prepare to help the program. However, these are not the kids to whom I would be offering that last spot or two. Those last spots are for those special kinds of kids I spoke of above. Those are the kids for whom the concept of offering them the options listed above makes sense. Plus, those special kids are often mature enough to be able to handle the responsibility that goes with being an eleventh or twelfth man.

Once a coach has created her team, she will have to find a way to get the kids who do make the team enough playing time to keep them interested and help them develop along the way. If a kid is sitting at the end of the bench, a coach has to figure out how to get that kid some time. It may mean moving her down to the next level, or it may mean swinging her between levels. It may mean the coach just has to make sure that the player gets into the rotation. Whatever it is, the coach needs to find the solution.

Players—Be a Participant in Your Own Rescue

Parents can help by reminding one of these eleventh or twelfth kids to be a part of the solution. Kid have to talk to their coach in the right setting about how they feel. They should ask what they need to do to get more time. They have to work at the things the coach tells them to work on. I often quote the whitewater rafting guide who told us as we were starting down the river, "If you fall out of the boat, be a participant in your own rescue." Kids need to do the same thing in sports, in school, and in life.

So often kids take the easy road and blame adults for their problems, instead of taking some responsibility. I sometimes would say to that player, "If you were as good as you think you are, why wouldn't I be playing you more? You are just not ready for many varsity minutes yet. You have not yet distinguished yourself the way you believe you have. So in order to get that time, you need to do the things that I am telling you to do." The kid can tell me what she thinks she is doing, and I can tell her how I see what she is doing. The key is there is an open line of communication. Unfortunately, kids don't always use that.

Notice, though, that there is no place in the communication above where the parent is involved. That's because if it is done right, the parent doesn't have to be involved. However, I know that at times these communications break down and need to go to another level, and that often involves the parents coming in to talk. But done correctly, it is done by first having the kid talk to the coach and then the parent coming in when necessary.

If that procedure is followed, then when the parent comes in, the coach can draw upon what has already been said to the player. The parents certainly have the right to know why their child isn't playing as much as they think she should be. The coach has the right to explain herself and show what the player is not doing to garner more playing time. If it is merely a lack of skills in certain areas, the coach needs to say that, but she needs to do so tactfully. To say, "Well, Julie really can't handle the ball and can't shoot. She also can't guard anyone to save her life," may be the blunt truth, but it certainly is not dignified. Coaches need to use tact when dealing with these issues, even when parents don't.

When the player's minimal playing time is due to a poor attitude, this too has to be communicated. Poor attitude issues must be handled with care. If we say, "Julie has a bad attitude," nothing is accomplished. We need to be specific, but again we must use tact. While it may be more difficult, it is far better to say, "Julie doesn't work as hard as she is capable of doing. Also, she is abrasive whenever I try to correct her or show her something. She complains too much to her teammates and often yells negative things at them. None of these things are good for the team or for Julie." Now a parent has something concrete to deal with. The parent can certainly address those statements by the coach. Even though these direct statements may be taken poorly by the parent, we coaches need to do this if we truly want to see our players improve and to foster good communication all around.

21 ❖ Breakdown of the Family Structure

The next area where parents have had a negative influence on youth sports is in what I would call a general breakdown of the family structure. With so many single parent and divorce situations in the United States today, kids have suffered. While kids have suffered in numerous ways, the way I will focus on is how it has affected their sports.

In the traditional stereotypical family, mom and dad were involved in their kids' lives by being there for them and supporting them in all aspects. Dad would "have a catch" with Junior after work. After Junior did his chores on Saturday morning, Dad would take him to the park in the afternoon to help him with his game or to drop him off to play whatever season's sport it was with his friends and without a coach. When Junior was old enough to play organized sports, both mom and dad would get him to practice or watch his games. However, if they couldn't make it to see every game, it was not a big deal. There would be other games to see. In Little League and Pop Warner Football (the only two non-school, youth sports offered at that time), Junior would get to play a fair amount of the time, even if Junior was not the best player on the team. Once Junior was in school athletics, if he made the team but didn't play a lot of minutes in games, Dad might go in to talk to the coach and ask why and find out what Junior could do to play more. Then Dad would try to carve out some time to help Junior with the skills he was lacking.

Well, that has all changed—some of it for the better, but mostly for the worse. In the new model, if Junior has two parents and knows them both, he is lucky to live with them both under the same roof. So many kids today see only one parent at a time. They are constantly learning discipline from two different people, at two different times, from two very different perspectives.

Too often, Junior is a pawn in the middle of the bitterness and resentment that his divorced parents have for one another. Instead of realizing that he is one of the few good things they did together and treating him so, he gets torn between the two of them. When he is being disciplined by one and then is spending time with the other, the other often does not carry out the discipline. "You say your dad only lets you stay up until 9:00? That's far too early for an eleven-year-old boy. Well, since you're eleven, with me you can stay up until 11:00."

Or maybe they actually do realize he is the one good thing they did together, so they often treat him like he can do no wrong, and discipline is a foreign concept to Junior. "After all," the dad might think, "if I can only see him so many hours, I don't want to spend my time with him being grounded. Then he might not like me, or worse yet, he might like mom more." And this is just one simple example of the numerous ways in which Junior's discipline is completely haywire. There is no consistency about it, and consistency is one of the most important elements of discipline and of a child's sense of security.

Now imagine Junior at soccer practice. The coach says to do something, and Junior doesn't want to do it. Coach repeats the command, and Junior half-heartedly goes through the motions. Coach tells Junior to take a lap. Junior does not understand. "Why should I do that? I don't want to. When my dad gets here, he'll talk to the coach for me." The dad always changes the discipline that the mom gives out. Why not do the same with Coach?

Now obviously, that may be an exaggeration, but it is not a stretch to see how torn a kid could be when it comes to receiving discipline from a coach. Junior is used to having two sets of rules and having someone always there to bail him out of what he doesn't want to do. Why should it be different in other places? As a teacher, I obviously think of the classroom situation first. How about at work? At a friend's house? At the mall? The list goes on and on.

Lack of Parent Interest

Another way that the breakdown of the family structure has hurt Junior is that both of his parents aren't nearly as involved in his life. It may be that both of them don't see his games, or only one of them does, and this becomes a double-edged sword. In the old model, parents sometimes missed games, but it was not a big deal because there would be other games to see. Nowadays, some parents never go to games, while others wouldn't dream of missing a game. Each one carries its own problems. The parent who never sees a game is hurting the child in immeasurable ways. The child takes it to mean, "What you value has no value to me. I just don't care about your life and what's important to you in it." Of course, parents don't usually verbalize this, and they probably don't even recognize this is the way it is viewed. But kids do. Kids pick up on all kinds of non-verbals that parents send out, whether the parent knowingly sends them out or not. Even if the single parent is holding two jobs and simply can't attend, the kid can't help but feeling slighted.

In education, both in sports and in school, we see too many instances of parents who are not at all involved in their kids' lives. The following quote is from an article called *Parents: Missing in Action!*: "For varying reasons, many children are growing up without the guidance they need to become productive members of society. Parents—most of whom do not realize it—are handicapping their children and sending them into this world ill-prepared and unbalanced."

I sure hope that if you are one of these parents, you take a long, hard look in the mirror and realize what you are doing to your kids. I hope you care enough for your kids to change this behavior and start showing more love and interest in what your kid does, whether it is sports, or math, or music, or whatever. Check out your kids' lives away from home. They need to know that you care about all aspects of their lives.

Overzealous Parents

Unfortunately, most of the parents discussed above aren't the ones reading this book. Most of the parents reading this book are already plugged into their kids' lives away from home. In fact, many of you reading this book are the ones who are on the flip side of this problem—who may be over-involved in your kids' lives. You are the ones who have to be at every game because if you weren't, "What would Junior do? He couldn't play without me there. He needs me!"

While I would much rather see a parent more involved in a kid's life than not at all involved, in many ways, the over-involved parent has become a bigger problem in youth athletics. When I spoke earlier of people who have said to me, "I could never be a coach; the parents would drive me crazy," these are the parents who these people are talking about.

In fact, other than the young parents new to youth sports who are worried about the journey upon which they are about to embark with their kids, it is the over-involved parents, more than anyone else, for whom I wrote this book. I knew that you would read this, because you are so involved in your kids' sports that you would have to find out what was wrong with them. Well, as we have said throughout this book, there are many problems. However, to be blunt, you are certainly one of the problems!

Congratulations to you if you haven't thrown this book down in disgust. Allow me to elaborate a bit. First of all, I am not saying that it is a problem if you want to attend all of your kids' games. It's interesting as I write this to note that when I started writing this book a few years ago, I did see that as a problem. While I was an athletic director, I saw so many parents who were so intense and almost insane about seeing their kids play their games, that I saw that as a huge problem. After having my own son playing his games for the last ten years, I get it now. There is nothing I enjoy doing more in my life than watching him play his games.

However, I am not rabid or insane about seeing my son play. I love to do it, but if I were to miss a game, I would live. I am also not acting up at the games that I do watch. I have released him to his game, and I try to just be a supportive, encouraging fan. Sure, I have my moments, but not like the people to whom I am referring as I describe the rabid, intense, insane fans.

I'm also not saying that overzealous parents are the biggest problem in youth sports. I don't think there is just one biggest problem. There are numerous issues that come to mind when considering what makes overzealous parents a problem. As listed before, some of these are the unrealistic expectations and pressures put on kids, warped perspectives of their kids' abilities, a gross amount of time and money spent on the sport, poor communications with coaches and administrators, and inappropriate behaviors, just to name a few. Let's look at each.

Unrealistic Expectations and Pressures

Parents often see their kid as being the best player on the team. Even when this is true, this can lead to problems for the child. If she sees herself that way because she is constantly hearing it from home, she may expect special treatment. No matter what sport the kid plays, overzealous parents who see their child as the best will tell the kid that since she is the best player, she should try to score more, or try to hit home runs more, or do anything more to be the star. This may be completely out of line with the philosophy or style the coach is trying to instill in the team, but that doesn't matter to these parents. If she is the best, she needs to be doing her own thing.

State Champs

A second expectation that is often unrealistic is that one's kids are going to be state champions (or whatever the ultimate championship is at the level they are playing). While I don't feel that winning is everything, it is certainly a big part of varsity sports, and it is good to have goals of winning championships. But so often, parents of kids

142

who are very good athletes place unrealistic expectations upon their kids and their teammates to achieve things that are extremely difficult. Athletes should have high expectations and lofty goals; however, parents often take this concept and throw it completely out of whack. Let me give you a personal example to help illustrate this.

In my four years as head coach at one school, we had an average girls' basketball team. We did some things well, but we struggled to win many games. I can say that with authority because I was the athletic director and head coach of the girls' team for those four years. From all I have been told, it was much the same before I was there. Oh, we made our improvements in my four years, but we did not "set the world on fire" with regards to scoreboard success.

The year after I resigned, though, we had a group of incoming freshmen that we knew were going to be very good. We watched them for the years leading up to high school, and we could tell they were going to be something special. They were destined for some success that this program had not had in a long, long time, if ever. Here is the problem. Their parents had been telling them that for years. These girls were told that they would be State Champions for years. Keep in mind that this school hadn't had a girls' team even go to the state tournament in years. And these parents were talking about state championships—that's plural!

In their freshmen year they went to state, but they did not place. In their sophomore year they took third place. In their junior year, they lost in the state championship game in overtime by two points. In their final year playing, they took second place again, after going undefeated for the first eighteen games of the season, and losing only once after that in the state championship game. They were a very good team through the years like everyone thought they would be. They were coached by one of the best coaches I have ever known. However, the multiple state championships that their parents, grandparents, and other community members anointed them with a long time ago did not happen. They were one of the best teams in the state for the last three years of their high-school careers. However, as I tried to explain to people prior to them entering the school, a lot can happen along the way, and our girls found that out over the years.

Many things can keep a team from achieving the ultimate success they seek. Our girls had three major obstacles they could not overcome. 1) They were so good, they didn't have to work or practice hard, and when a great team showed up in the championship, they weren't prepared. 2) Petty jealousies and infighting caused a major break in their team chemistry. These jealousies were fueled by their parents. 3) The pressure these kids had on them from their parents for four years was more than most adults could handle, let alone 15-to-18-year-olds.

Again, it is good for kids to set the bar high for themselves. Unfortunately, these girls never had a chance to do that—Mommy and Daddy had done that for them and for all of their teammates. During their middle-school years, these girls won games by upwards of forty points. But it got to the point where, if they didn't win by double-digit margins, the kids were disappointed and their parents were wondering what was wrong. More importantly, there was a key ingredient missing in these girls' games—fun. They had so much pressure on them to win and to win big that they didn't look like they were having any fun at all.

Well, it's no wonder. During the game their parents were always yelling at them what to do, or they were mouthing and gesturing what to do when the girls looked into the stands. The girls' coach in middle school, by the way, was the very same outstanding coach who went on to coach them in high school. When I resigned my position as varsity head coach, I knew he was going to take over.

Prior to coaching at our middle school, he was a very successful varsity boys' coach at the high-school level, so I knew he would do well with the girls. Unfortunately, his biggest problem came from some of the parents. Here we had a great, well-respected coach coaching a group of seventh-and-eighth-grade girls to win after win after win, and the girls' parents were telling the girls what to do during the games. Then, after the games, one parent would pull his daughter aside to the basket to start showing her what she needed to be doing while another one was telling his daughter how terribly she played and another one was telling his girl that she should have shot the ball more.

The worst thing about all of the above is that over the course of their four years in high school, these middle-school girls grew into high school girls with all that comes with the territory. Boyfriends, jealousies over teammates' success, and classic girl/boy relationship infighting seeped into this team and caused some problems. The innocence was well on its way to being lost when things finally came to a head the summer before their senior year. Yes, that's right—over the summer. And unfortunately, it didn't come to a head with two players; it was with two parents.

After an exciting game at a tournament that our school was hosting that summer, the fathers of two of the girls on the team got into a knock-down drag-out fist fight with each other in the school parking lot in front of all the fans and kids. It was the pinnacle of how bad athletes' parents can become. It was an embarrassment to the girls, the team, and the community. Amazingly, the team rose above the idiocy that took place, but it required a meeting with all the kids and parents during the volleyball season to get everyone back on the same page. Well, that's not completely true. You see, not ALL of the parents showed up. In fact, two of the most important sets of parents didn't show up, and it really hurt the girls. They just wanted the opportunity to tell the parents they wanted everyone to work to get along for the rest of the volleyball season, and then through the upcoming basketball season. Fortunately, for the most part, people were able to do that.

However, it was interesting to find out after the season how much more was going on behind-the-scenes that the coach or I never knew about. The number of times throughout the season that the coach would have a parent stop by to "chat" or he would receive a call from one of them in which the parent would be complaining about one of his or her daughter's teammates are too many to mention in this book. The rumors of two or three kids breaking training rules late in the season came out during the playoffs, and while they were never proven true, they were never denied, either.

Then, after the season, one of the college coaches recruiting three of the girls told our head coach she had no idea how he was able to hold the team together well enough to have the success they had. She told him that EVERY TIME she came to our gym to watch the girls play, whether at games or practice, she had different parents come up to her to tout the strengths of their own daughters and to criticize and rip their daughter's teammates. Unbelievable! It's one thing to be so warped and overzealous that you go talk to a college coach about how great your little darling is. It's quite another to be so jaded that you would actually hurt someone else's chances of playing at the next level. That is just sick.

It is truly a shame. These girls were really good kids, and we loved having them in our programs for those four years. For the most part, especially up until late in their last season together, they showed others how we want our athletes to be (except for the jealousies and in-fighting). However, the coach, administrators, teachers, and I were happy to see all of this strife and tension come to an end.

The constant battle that we waged to keep them together took its toll on many people, especially our coach, whose health suffered during their last three years together. While he had to deal with the strong personalities of the girls, without question, one of the biggest contributors to the constant battle were the overzealous, over-involved parents that he had to deal with. It is a great lesson for others to learn about backing off and letting your kids have the experience to themselves. Bruce Brown, in his book, *Teaching Character Through Sport*, calls this "releasing them to the game," and it is exactly what they need. Kids need their parents to be supportive and be great fans, but to let them have the experience themselves when it comes to the games they play.

College Scholarships

Another unrealistic pressure that parents place upon their kids is the expectation of getting a college scholarship. This way of thinking has reached almost epidemic proportions. More and more parents are seeking college scholarships for their children. We tell parents all the time that if they want their kids to get a college scholarship, they should take them to the library more instead of the gym because the odds of getting an academic scholarship are far greater than the odds of getting an athletic scholarship.

But that is not the dream that so many parents have for their kids. The dream is that one day they will see their boy or girl playing on national television in front of millions of people. Well, that possibility is even more remote. It is time for parents to look at the numbers and do the math. Scholarshipstats.com points out how difficult the odds are of a high-school athlete playing a college sport, let alone receiving a scholarship to do so. An example of some of those statistics can be found at the NCAA's "Estimated Probability of Competing in College Athletics" report from April of 2018.

For instance, 3.4% of boys who played basketball in high school played at any level in college and only 1% played in each of the Division 1 and Division 2 levels. For girls who played basketball in high school 3.8% played in college, with only 1.2% playing Division 1 and 1.1% playing at the Division 2 level. For a complete listing for all of the sports in both genders go to the link at www.ncaa.org/about/resources/research/estimated-probability-competing-college-athletics.

Now I don't mean to quell a kid's dream or even the parents' dream. They need to dream big and do all they can to achieve their dreams. However, they must also be realistic about the odds. Also, they must remember that while they may have that dream and may be seeking it, their child is on a middle-school or high-school team that has other goals and desires than just this one player getting a college scholarship. As long as Junior or Junior's dad's dream does not interfere with the goals of the team, then it is okay to go for that dream. But the moment that the dream becomes detrimental to the team and the program, we have a problem.

Parents must remember that coaches are there to help kids have a positive experience in this school—all kids, not just the ones with future athletic aspirations. Our focus is on the here and now. Oh sure, we are trying to build our programs and the future of the programs. But it is our programs we are trying to build, not the colleges' programs. If your kid is good enough to get an athletic scholarship, colleges will find her or him. As coaches, we will certainly help in the process, but it will not be our focus and as parents, it shouldn't be yours.

In fact, college coaches struggle with recruiting players whose parents are so heavily involved in the process. Don't worry. They will talk with parents during the process. But they want to be the ones doing the calling and contacting, not you. They get very gun-shy and put out by parents who are too pushy and overbearing. Recently, I have been told of college coaches who have stopped recruiting certain kids because of how those kids' parents were already becoming a problem. These players are not even at the school yet, and their parents were pushing too much, so the coach stopped the recruiting process. I have also been told of a college volleyball coach who now recruits so as to keep 15 players on her team, planning to have to get rid of two or three due to parents becoming too involved in the program, with the coach, and with the player's life at college. What a shame that it has come to this. Parents have always been a problem for youth, middle-school, and high-school coaches. But college coaches? This is new territory that we are venturing into.

Even newer territory, though, was ventured into in 2016. We watched LaVar Ball, the father of three very good basketball players, got way too involved in all three of his kids' basketball careers. The oldest son Lonzo had a great year with the UCLA Bruins, and he was slated to be picked as a very high draft pick for the NBA. LaVar was out on many talk shows touting his son's skills and all that he would bring to an NBA team. Lonzo was chosen by the Los Angeles Lakers with the 2nd pick, and LaVar doubled down on all of his bombastic predictions. When Lonzo struggled during his rookie year, LaVar did what many high school parents do—he criticized the coach publicly.

LaVar's middle child, LeAngelo, was also playing basketball for UCLA at the time. LeAngelo got into an international legal incident while on a team trip to China, and he was disciplined by the team and the school. LaVar pulled him out of school and took him and the third brother, LaMelo, who was a junior in high school, out of the country to play professionally. Neither boy can now play collegiately because they lost their amateur status. Therefore, their only future options are foreign professional leagues, lower level professional leagues in the US, or the NBA if an NBA team believes they are good enough to draft them.

It is a shame what this parent has done. I hope his kids can rise above some of the antics and behaviors he displayed. While I'm sure he loves his boys, and he means well and wants nothing but the best for them, he went way overboard in his handling of them. Fortunately, as I write this, Lonzo is having a good start to his second year with the Los Angeles Lakers. Hopefully, that will continue, and hopefully, the two younger boys will be able to realize their dreams of playing in the NBA, as well. But a lot of people are rooting against all of them, all because of how their dad handled their situations.

So parents, let your kid's actions in their competitive arenas create the interest from the colleges and pros—not your letters, phone calls, highlight videos, tweets, posts, and interviews. Then once they are there, release them to the game and to their coaches, like you were supposed to release them when they were younger.

If your child is a good enough athlete to play at the next level and you have the financial means to do so, you might consider checking out one of the many recruiting services out there now. These can be a helpful way to get your child's name and abilities in front of college coaches. But be careful. Some of them are merely lining their pockets with your hard-earned dollars. Do your research. Ask for your child's high-school coach's input about this. The reason why using one of these services might be a good choice is that they can put together a professionally done package on your child. It also takes some of that extra work off the coach's plate. It is also not coming from you, but from a professional (hopefully) organization. Again though, tread carefully when choosing to do this.

*NOTE—For all my years as a head coach, I was wary of these organizations, and with good reason. However, in my own son's recruiting process the last couple of years, we found NCSA—Next College Student Athlete. They have been a very helpful organization, and from all I can tell are doing right by kids. We have been very happy with their service so far. My son is a senior, so we will see where he lands, but NCSA has been a huge part of the process going as well as it has so far.

Warped Perspectives

Parents often have warped perspectives of their kids' abilities. The parent who sees his kid getting a college scholarship when his kid is an average high-school player at best falls into this category. In many instances, this is deeply ingrained. I have a 17-year-old boy. I think he has some decent athletic ability. Is he a great athlete? I don't know. So far, he has been pretty good, and he would at least be considered a good athlete and great teammate. However, I have to guard against my thinking that way too much, or else I will start to believe he can do things that he actually can't—or may not want to.

It has been the same with him in the classroom. He gets good grades, and throughout his life, teachers have said that he is fairly advanced. My wife and I would beam with pride every time we would hear examples of what he was doing that was so advanced. However, we realized that we must watch out, because these were merely the opinions of what his teachers thought he was capable of becoming. He has continued to excel in high school, but the road has been much harder the further along he has gone. Still, he is ranked in the top 10 of his class of 120, so he continues to excel, but we don't want to assume anything. We will see where it takes him, but we are also realistic. Time will tell what kind of student and athlete he ends up being.

This is the problem too many parents have and then can't let go of. They see and hear their children do wonderful things at an early age and start to buy into the concept that they are gifted. Then as the rest of the world catches up to the kids, the parents lose sight of that. When they are young, there is nothing that their kid can't do. Again, I don't mean to quell kids' or parents' dreams. They need to shoot for the stars while being realistic about those dreams. Kids need to believe they can be astronauts, or baseball players, or the President of the United States, if that's what they want. Other people have become those things, so why not them? And we must show them how to achieve those things. However, we must also show them what the odds are and what else they can do that might provide similar joy if the dream does not work out. If their talents are honed with training and hard work, great things will come of it.

I am a fifty-something year-old adult and I have dreams. I hope that this book will be published and then sell a lot of copies, and due to that, I hope to help fix some of the problems with athletics in our world. I then hope to be able to continue to write and speak full-time, and then live out the rest of my days in my dream home on my dream property.

That is my dream and has been for a long time. It has not happened yet, but I am still seeking it. I don't want anyone telling me it can't or won't happen. I need people to encourage me that it can happen, so I keep on pushing on toward my goal. At the same time, I am staying realistic about it. All of our dreams don't come true, but I have seen enough of the world to know that if you don't have dreams, you will never achieve big things in life. So I dream, but I dream with perspective.

Kids need to be encouraged to do the same. Dream big, and go for it. Parents need to be the encouragers, but they also need to be the pragmatists who help their kids move in the directions of their dreams, while realizing that their kids may not achieve those dreams. That doesn't mean that they tell their children, "Why are you trying that? Do you know hard it is to be an NBA player?"

Rather, the parent needs to say, "You know, I am so excited that you want to make it to the NBA. I will hold the vision with you of seeing you play there someday. However, for you to make it there, it is going to take an awful lot more hard work than you are doing at this time. I'm willing to help you try to get there if you want. But you also need to understand that it might not happen, and that's okay, too. All that hard work will pay off, and there will be other opportunities for you along the way. I just want you to know that whatever you want to do in life, I'm here for you. I'm here to help. Let me know what I can do, and if I am capable of doing it, I will." This parent is trying to encourage her kid, while at the same time letting her kid know that the dream may not happen, which is okay, too. This is a much healthier situation than the parent who says it can't be done. Any big-dreaming child will encounter enough naysayers along the way.

The other side, of course, is the parent who is so warped that he sees no other end in sight but the dream coming true. This parent is dangerous because his focus blinds him to the reality of the situation. He is the "me" who could have been thinking a few years back that my boy, before he ever left middle school, will be playing for Coach K at Duke some day. I have dealt with these parents throughout my years of coaching. They end up creating all kinds of pressure for their kid that the kid should have never had to face. They also set them up for failure down the road because if the child doesn't live up to the expectations, then the child will feel like a failure.

The biggest problem with this parent is that this warped perspective clouds the parent's judgment and then leads to the parent doing and saying outrageous things. These actions and words can be directed at the coach, the officials, other school personnel, college coaches or scouts, the player's teammates, or the player himself. It can be telling the coach that Junior needs to shoot more or telling Junior's teammates that they need to get the ball to Junior more. It could be yelling at the officials every time Junior makes a mistake, so as to make it look like Junior didn't make the obvious mistake he just made. It could be sending, or worse yet bringing in person, a highlight tape of all of Junior's accomplishments to a college coach who has not shown any interest in Junior before.

A parent with a warped perspective usually is blinded to the truth and often acts in such a manner that is hurtful and embarrassing to the child. While the parent's intent is never to be hurtful or embarrassing, this is what often happens with this type of parent. As I discussed earlier, parents need to "release their kids to the games" that they play.

Time, Injuries, Food, and Money

Overzealous parents often spend an inordinate amount of time and money on their kids' sports. Nowadays, parents will get their kids onto multiple teams at the same time—some in different sports, some in the same sport. Or they will hire a personal trainer or coach to work with their kid. Often, they are trying to create an opportunity to get that college scholarship. This creates all kinds of time, stress, health, and commitment issues for the kids. Junior is often racing off from one practice, game, or tournament to another. His time is so consumed, he has little or no time for homework or the fun things in life.

Sports-medicine doctors and physical therapists are saying that overuse injuries account for the biggest increase in injuries they've seen over the last 15-to-20 years—many from kids playing multiple sports in one season, or from playing on multiple teams of the same sport in one season, or from playing or training for one sport year-round with no real rest. The classics are basketball, volleyball, soccer, and baseball, but quite honestly, any sport can create this problem. Kids are often playing for their school team in one sport and then playing AAU or club for the same or another sport, with multiple practices and games on the same days. Their young bodies never have the chance to recuperate. It used to be that between school seasons (football, basketball, baseball), there was usually a week or two for the body and spirit to rest and regenerate. Now, school seasons often go right up against each other and even overlap, not to mention the club and AAU seasons taking up that time as well.

Dr. James Andrews is a leading authority on sports-related injuries. He has practiced medicine for nearly 40 years and is most famous for his ability to put professional athletes back together. In 2010, Andrews was the only doctor to be named among the top-40 most powerful people in the NFL by *Sports Illustrated*. Dr. Andrews describes the situation, with some advice for parents, as follows:

I started seeing a sharp increase in youth-sports injuries, particularly baseball, beginning around 2000. I started tracking and researching, and what we've seen is a five- to-sevenfold increase in injury rates in youth sports across the board. I'm trying to help these kids, given the epidemic of injuries that we're seeing. That's sort of my mission: to keep them on the playing field and out of the operating room. I hate to see the kids that we used to not see get hurt. Now they're coming in with adult, mature-type sports injuries. It's a real mess.

Specialization leads to playing the sport year-round. That means not only an increase in risk factors for traumatic injuries but also a sky-high increase in overuse injuries. Almost half of sports injuries in adolescents stem from overuse.

Professionalism is taking these kids at a young age and trying to work them as if they are pro athletes, in terms of training and year-round activity. Some can do it, like Tiger Woods. He was treated like a professional golfer when he was 4, 5 and 6 years old. But you've got to realize that Tiger Woods is a special case. A lot of these kids don't have the ability to withstand that type of training and that type of parental/coach pressure.

The first thing I would tell them is, their kid needs at least two months off each year to recover from a specific sport. Example: youth baseball. For at least two months, preferably three-to-four months, they don't need to do any kind of overhead throwing, any kind of overhead sport, and let the body recover in order to avoid overuse situations. That's why we're seeing so many Tommy John procedures, which is an adult operation designed for professionals. In my practice now, 30 to 40 percent of the ones I'm doing are on high-schoolers, even down to ages 12 or 13. They're already coming in with torn ligaments. Please! Give them time off to recover.

The above excerpts are from Dennis Manoloff's article in *The Plain Dealer* (see Bibliography). For more in-depth ideas from Dr.

Andrews, check out his book, *Any Given Monday: Sports Injuries and How to Prevent Them, for Athletes, Parents and Coaches—Based on My Life in Sports Medicine* (Scribner).

Another health issue related to all of this extra time the parents are having the kids put in is their nutrition. Kids will often have to wolf down some fast food in the car on their way from one practice to another. On numerous weekends of the year, these kids are playing in tournaments where they eat nachos, hot dogs, and pop. I understand that kids eat these things regularly, but when a family spends two evenings a week going from one practice to another and then Saturday and Sunday at the gym all day, how well is Junior's body being fueled? And let's face it—Junior's body is being asked to do a whole lot more than other kids, so he needs better nutrition. When you look at the amount of time spent playing the sports and the kind of fuel going into these kids' bodies, it's no wonder that their bodies are breaking down.

Money is another factor that parents are going way overboard on when it comes to these sports. As just mentioned, parents are spending a lot on fast food for their kids, but that's just a small part of it. Junior needs new shoes for every season, which can run $100–$200 a pair. Also, he needs a new uniform for these club teams, which can be in the $50–$75 range. To be on the team, kids may need to pay a fee from $200 to $500, or higher. If a parent decides to hire a personal trainer or coach for the child, that will be anywhere from $25 to $75 per hour. Many tournaments are a long way from home, so you have the cost of gasoline, hotel rooms and meals, plus the cost for the family to get into the tournament. In the summertime, kids go away to sport-specific camps that can cost $250 to $750 per camp. All of it adds up to a lot of money for families, all in the name of getting Junior more opportunities to play.

Dr. Andrews addressed the money aspect of kids sports, too:

> The almighty dollar has a lot to do with it, yes. Some parents are putting a football or baseball in their kids' hands when they're 3 years old, and it's not just for a fun little

photograph. Parents are projecting 10, 12 years. Don't get me wrong, I'm for sports. I love sports. I want these kids to reach their full potential, and if the potential is a college scholarship, great. If it's a pro career, great. But to think they're all going to be professional athletes is misguided. The odds against it are so very, very high. Even the ones who get college scholarships comprise a much smaller percentage than parents think. (Manoloff)

22 ❖ Poor Communications with Coaches & Admin

While it is imperative for parents and coaches to communicate, how they communicate is critical. Too often there is no communication whatsoever between parents and coaches. Coaches need to be proactive in establishing a line of communication with parents. This is often difficult and stressful. It is much easier to avoid parents than to actively seek them out. I have been guilty of this every year I have coached. Rather than go talk to a parent of a kid with whom I was having a problem, I would choose to avoid that parent. Invariably that behavior created or added to more problems down the road.

In fact, a few years ago my athletic director pointed out to me that I really needed to do a better job of making sure people knew I was approachable. While every year I tell parents and kids that I am happy to meet with them and discuss any situations or concerns they may have, I guess my actions and my words didn't match. So one of my major focuses has become to make sure people know they can approach me. As I started to meet more with people wanting to talk, or offer suggestions or concerns, I found that, no matter the situation, it has usually had positive consequences, and I felt better about having done so.

On the other side of the equation are parents who will not talk to the coach, or will do so only to complain about something. Coaches are teachers, too, and should be afforded a similar type of respect, as in the parent/teacher meetings, done in a "sit-down, let's work this out" kind of atmosphere. Everyone is trying to help kids have the best possible chance for success, and we just need to figure out how to help them get there.

When parents meet with coaches, though, it sometimes takes on an "anything goes" attitude. Parents will come up to the coach before, during or after a practice or a game, in the gym, in the parking lot, at the grocery store, on the phone, or anywhere else that they feel is okay for them. Coaches tend to feel that they are being "jumped" when this happens, which creates a feeling of anxiety and defensiveness on the coach's part. He has no idea where this conversation is headed, and he has done nothing to prepare for it. In a parent/teacher conference, the teacher gets prepared by pulling out the student's work, the grade book, and any notes that he has taken about the student. He is ready to help the parent understand what's going on. Then together, they discuss what can be done to help the student.

But when a parent just comes at a coach in any of the settings mentioned above, the coach has no chance to prepare for the meeting and formulate some ideas as to how we can help Junior have a better experience on this team. All the coach is thinking is, "I gotta' get out of here." That's because the coach does not feel he is being dealt with on a level playing field.

So, parents, call the school or the coach directly to set up a time to meet that is convenient for both of you. In most cases, I think it's better to have the player there as well. After all, she is the one the whole meeting is about. She needs to hear what is being said. So often what Mom and Dad hear at home is not what was said or what happened at school. Not that she is lying about it—although that happens, too—but how it was interpreted by her, and then how it was interpreted by Mom and Dad can come off vastly different than how it was meant or expressed by the coach. However, if what you are discussing is too personal or sensitive, then the player doesn't have to be there.

Also, whether the player is going to be at the meeting or not, talk to her first. Find out how she feels about the situation. If she doesn't have a problem with the coach or the situation, why should the parent? I have seen parents come in to talk with a coach where it was only the parent who had the problem.

In one meeting I was involved in as the athletic director, it took a half hour of back-and-forth bantering between the parent and coach for the parent to finally admit that his son didn't have a problem with the coach or how much he played. It was just that the dad couldn't accept that his kid was playing so little. The kid understood his role on the team; the dad didn't.

Even after admitting that, the dad still went to the superintendent of the school district to complain about the coach and how little his son played. His son ended up choosing to play on the JV for the rest of the season, so he could play more minutes. He was fine with that. On his Senior Night, his dad refused to even come to the game and walk out on the court with his son while he was being honored. It was his way of showing the coach that he still disagreed with the way things went. That was the biggest shame of the entire situation. All it showed was how misguided this dad was with his feelings. Imagine not walking out on the basketball court with your son at his last home game ever because you have a problem with his coach. Unfortunately, your son would always remember that you didn't walk out with him on his Senior Night.

Guidelines for Meeting with the Coach

Here are some guidelines for a parent meeting with a coach. You should sit down in an office or a classroom. Look the coach in the eye and express your concerns in a calm demeanor. Ask questions and offer insights, but by all means, remain calm throughout the meeting, and allow the coach the opportunity to answer. Remember that both of you want your child to have a positive athletic experience. It's just that each of you may have different ideas about what that means or about how to get there. Avoid the urge to interrupt. Take notes to prepare for a future question or to ask for clarification.

As you discuss your child's situation, keep in mind why you are there. This is not about winning an argument—it's about finding out what your kid needs to do to improve his situation to have a positive experience on his team. Again, if you have spoken with him about this beforehand, it will make it a lot easier to express your concerns. If, for instance, you are talking about football playing time as key to his positive experience, but he doesn't want to be the receiver, only the quarterback, then your discussion is going nowhere.

The coach also needs to keep in mind that this is not about winning an argument. However, the coach's dynamic is different than the parents' dynamic. He is trying to provide a positive experience for all players, not just the parents' kid. And quite honestly, it is usually the parents of the last couple of kids on the bench who come in complaining. Still, all parents are wanting a positive experience for their kids. It's just that what constitutes a positive experience may be different for each.

Another dynamic that the coach is dealing with is that he is trying to win games, especially if he is a varsity head coach. Sometimes, winning games and playing time for your child are going to oppose each other. Your child may be good enough to be on the team and get a few minutes here and there, but she still needs a lot of work to get a lot of minutes. That's why we often like to swing players between levels. This gives them a taste of what it is like at the varsity level, but they also get a lot of minutes of playing time on a lower level to keep developing their skills. I know it is sometimes difficult on a kid to be a swing player, but it can be hugely beneficial. Otherwise, that kid doesn't play much, or only plays against much weaker competition and is then not as well-prepared for the level of play when she actually does play on varsity.

Once you have gotten all of your points expressed and the coach has addressed them all, thank the coach for allowing you the opportunity to talk. It may be that you have resolved the issue right there. It may be that it was an issue that merely needed to be explained and heard, and only time will tell how it plays out. Whatever the case may be, allow the coach and your child the chance to work through whatever the situation was and recognize that change may take a while. Be supportive of both your child and the coach. Don't measure every decision and every situation by how your meeting went. There is a lot more going on than just your situation.

If after a few weeks, you still don't see any changes in behavior, you may want to contact the coach again and also contact the athletic director. Keep in mind, though, that while you may not see change, there may actually be change. Again, one of the best ways to figure that out is to talk to your child about it. S/he will probably be able to enlighten you as much as the coach. However, if not, then set up another meeting. This time, have the athletic director be a part of the meeting.

The AD can then try to mediate any conflict that there may be. He or she can also try to work with the coach to help resolve the issue. If the AD does not see that the coach has a problem, then s/he will try to work with the parents to get them to see the situation a little more realistically. Emotions can cloud our judgments. These are our babies that the coaches are dealing with, and it is difficult to be completely objective. Coaches have emotions, too. So the AD will try to understand both sides from a more objective point of view.

Hopefully, this second meeting will bring some resolution, but if not, a parent can continue up the chain to the principal, the superintendent, and the school board. Understand though, that the further up you go, the more serious the issue becomes. These people don't need to be bothered with the fact that you think Junior needs to be playing more. If you bring this type of an issue to these administrators, you are often not going to get very far, and in the future, it will be harder for them to take you seriously with other issues you may have. Unfortunately, you have just become one of "those parents." If however, your concern is about how the coach is treating kids, or that the coach is taking money from the fundraisers, or the coach is not looking out for the safety of the kids, or some other serious problem, you certainly should bring this up the chain of command as far as necessary.

Notice, though, that scheduled meetings are always used to resolve these problems, not random, on-the-spot encounters. When parents follow the procedure correctly, coaches and administrators rarely have a problem with parents.

23 ❖ Living Vicariously Through Kids

Parents will sometimes live vicariously through their kids, especially in sports. If the parents never made it big in sports, they may feel that their kids might make it. The parent can then experience what they missed out on.

There are a few problems with doing this. First, they put undue pressure upon their children. They are always pushing their kids to achieve at the next level. They never allow their kids to just be the best they are right now. There is always something greater to shoot for.

As with so many things in athletics, there is a fine line here. You want kids to keep raising the bar, to keep working to achieve and to improve, but they should be doing it for themselves and their team-mates and their own goals, not for you. This works the same way as when we spoke of parents trying to get their kids college scholarships. If the child has a goal of getting a college scholarship, that's one thing. But when the parent is the one pushing the idea of a college scholarship, not only does it create a warped perspective for the parent, but it also puts added pressure on the kid.

In fact, getting a college scholarship is one way that parents live vicariously through their children. That's a big mistake. I don't think parents should even talk about athletic scholarships with their kids unless the kids bring them up. Then make sure to tell them about the odds of getting an athletic scholarship, versus the odds of getting an academic scholarship. As of this writing, the ratio of academic scholarships to athletic scholarships is about 75:1.

Make sure your kids know that they do not HAVE to get an athletic scholarship for them to get to college. Tell them that you will find a way to make sure they get there if they really want to go to college. If you are not talking about them getting an athletic scholarship, hopefully they won't feel pressure to get one. Let's face it. If your child is a really good athlete, other people will already be talking with her or him about getting a college scholarship, so the pressure will already be great enough that s/he doesn't need Mom and Dad fueling the fire.

Another way that parents live vicariously through their kids is focusing on their statistics and on winning. Please, don't do this. I have seen too many parents out there who sit in the stands and keep track of their kid's statistics. Let me explain why I think this is a huge problem. First, individual statistical accomplishments are not the goal of the team or of the coach. When you focus on your kid's statistics, you are creating a "me-first" mentality with your child. Now it becomes all about his or her points, goals, assists, rebounds, etc. as opposed to the team's success. Second, the coach is trying to instill all kinds of goals into a team, many of which have nothing to do with statistics. When you start focusing on your child's statistics, you start chipping away at the team itself. Third, there are many forms of success that a team measures itself by, not just winning and losing and not just individual statistics. Let the coach determine what individual accomplishments the team and the players should hear and know about.

Then again, what age kid are we talking about? When I had a varsity boys' basketball player's dad in the stands with a little notebook keeping track of his son's points and rebounds, that was bad enough. But how about the parent of a fourth grader at an AAU game tallying her points and free throws? Why are they doing this? What good could this possibly bring about? I can only see problems. You are headed down a road toward creating a selfish, me-first, individual, who feels all kinds of pressure to perform well, as opposed to an unselfish, team-first teammate who plays the game for the fun of it. Which of those two would you rather play with, if you were a kid on her team? So, I would ask parents to help their kid help their team and future teams. Put away the pencil and paper. Go cheer and support her and her team by being a positive role model as a supportive fan.

Finally, parents often live vicariously through their children because of their own feelings of inadequacy or lack of success. What a huge burden to put upon your kids. Parents, don't let your kid's success or failure be your barometer of your own success or failure. When your kid misses the game-winning free throw, don't bury your head in your hands in shame. Sit tall and keep your head up. When the time is right and he is ready to talk, you should say something like, "That's okay. You gave it your best, son. At least you were out there in the arena giving it your all. We just love watching you play. We're still very proud of you, and we love you very much."

Don't show him that you are embarrassed, ashamed, or upset. That is not what he needs, nor is it what you need to show everyone else, either. When you stand tall and show him that it's okay that he failed and that you are still proud of him, you help him understand how he should react, too. If you are full of shame at failure, how would you expect him to react? He's going to hurt, that's for sure, but he needs to know that it's okay to fail. He may not need you to hold his hand or hug him right now, but he needs your support in whatever way he likes best.

So much of what happens in athletics is experiencing public failure. It is amazing when you think about how well kids deal with this for the most part. They risk failure every time they play their games, and they are doing so in public with many, many people watching them. One of the great things about sports is that it is a place where we can teach young people to risk failure, to fail, and to come back again and again. What is the result? Yes, there's some hurt, frustration and self-doubt, but there is usually some growth, development of resiliency, and other qualities that will help the next time they are in this situation again. What a great arena to learn the lessons of failing and bouncing back. There are worse places where kids may learn about failure—academics, driving, alcohol, drugs, sex, run-ins with the law—from which the consequences may be far more serious.

It is often tough not to live vicariously through our kids. Isn't the classic parenting line, I just want my kids to have what I never had? That is a setup for vicarious living if I ever heard one. Parents should want their kid to have what the kid wants, rather than what the parents never had. So, as you try to provide your kid a better life, make sure it's his or her life you are trying to make better, not yours.

24 ❖ Poor Sportsmanship

Some of the poorest sportsmanship we see at games comes from the parents of the kids playing in those games. I believe this has become an epidemic in American athletics, and it is what is ruining our games more than anything else. If we don't get a handle on this soon, we are going to have major problems in the future. Actually, we already do. I first wrote the first three lines of this paragraph over ten years ago. The behavior of parents at youth athletic contests has always been suspect, but in the last ten to fifteen years, the headlines have continued to get scarier.

As an athletic director, there was no bigger concern that I always had in the back of my mind than fan (mostly parent) behavior at games. It's usually not the kids in the crowd who are the biggest problem. What a sad commentary. Oh sure, we have to deal with some rowdy kids occasionally, but you expect some of that. They look at the college games on TV and see the "Cameron Crazies" or some other group of college fans doing some wild things, and they want to be just like them. When we tell them they have to stop whatever it is they're doing, they usually stop, and we don't have another problem.

However, the parents are a different story. Now keep in mind, I am not talking about all parents. Many parents behave themselves in perfectly fine fashion. I'm talking about the ones who feel they can say and do almost anything they want. They will yell almost anything with no regard for anyone else's feelings. It is as if they feel a sense of entitlement because they paid their money, and that is their baby out there. They seem to have no concern for the people sitting around them, the players, the coaches, the officials, little kids, school personnel, or anyone else. It doesn't matter what sport, or what level the game is being played, whether it's third grade AAU or high-school varsity, or whether it's boys or girls. All that matters to them is that some perceived injustice is going on. This behavior can be directed toward a myriad of targets. Let's look at some of those behaviors and where they are directed.

Officials

While I addressed some of the following points about officials earlier in the section on coaches, this section for parents and fans bears some repeating. First, you have the parents who yell about every call made by an official that the parents believe were incorrect. Without a doubt, these are the most common offenses and often the worst. Walk into any gym in America where there is a basketball game being played, and I can guarantee you will hear someone complaining about the officiating, usually from fans of both teams. Of course, this problem is not in basketball alone, but basketball is a great example of how bad it gets. It doesn't matter if this is a second-grade youth league game or a high-school state championship. Parents sit in the stands and yell out at the officials all game long. No wonder we are losing officials at an alarming rate. Who wants to deal with that kind of abuse?

These officials are often young college kids who are trying to make a buck and trying to learn the ropes of officiating. They are inexperienced, and they are trying to learn how to do this, just like the kids for whom they are officiating. Now some know-it-all is yelling at them about every time a kid traveled and he didn't call it.

Our high-school leagues use these other leagues as training grounds for new officials to get some experience. Unfortunately, what often happens is the new officials deal with so much abuse from parental fans that they say, "To heck with this. If it's this bad at this level, I'm sure it's going to be worse as I move up." So they quit. They rarely move on. Who can blame them? Or they do move on and try the next level and realize they were right—it is worse at the high-school level, because you have even more know-it-alls in the stands. The further up the ladder of competition you go, the worse the problem gets, because there is more at stake and the emotions of everyone in the gym are more intense. Championships, scholarships, and jobs are on the line. Each possession becomes a life-or-death struggle. In a packed gym, it can get downright crazy.

Now I am exaggerating a bit when I say it becomes a life-or-death struggle, and yet, we have seen our share of headlines where officials have been beaten up and, yes, even killed after a game, where fans (or coaches) felt the officials did an injustice to their team. It amazes me how parents sitting one hundred feet away from the action will yell at officials standing four feet away from the action. Of course, the parents feel they saw it properly and have to let the official know, but come on! Do you really think if the official saw it the way you did that he would have made the call the way he did? He is a human being who had an interpretation of something he saw that was different than what you saw. Why do you feel you have to yell at him every time he saw something different? Why not just have him blow the whistle when something happens, stop the game, and turn to the crowd and take a vote? That would be the most democratic way, wouldn't it?

The problem is he is paid to officiate the game the way "he" sees it, not the way "we" see it. He is part of the game; we are not. He is a human being; he will make mistakes. So will the players and so will the coach. They are all human, and they go into the contest understanding that each one of them will make mistakes. Unfortunately, fans often forget this, especially when it comes to the officials. They expect some sort of infallible judge who sees everything perfectly and makes the right decision every time. Sorry, but in all of my years of life, I have yet to meet that person. And neither have any of those fans who expect that. So recognize that some mistakes are going to be made. Go ahead and gasp and say, "Shoot," or whatever it is you say when something doesn't go your way and then get over it. If there is truly some gross injustice occurring, the coach will address it with the official. That is part of his role in the game, not yours.

Coaches

The next group of people who have to deal with parental poor sportsmanship are coaches. It's amazing to me how many parents will say to me they could never coach because the parents would drive them nuts. Poor sportsmanship towards coaches comes in a few ways. Most often, it is directed at the coach of their player. When a coach makes a decision that a parent doesn't like and the parent yells out, "Come on, Coach. What are you doing?" or something like that, it is a show of poor sportsmanship.

Think about it. Imagine being at your job. As you are working, a group of people that has nothing to do with your work is watching you. When you make some move to do something, someone in this group yells out at you, "Come on, what are you doing?" Is that in good taste? Is that the work environment you want to try to make your living in? Is that going to help you be a better worker? I doubt it. Yet, our coaches (and officials) work under this type of scrutiny every game. And they do it, not in front of a small group of people, but often in front of hundreds or even thousands of people. What gives people the feeling that they have the right to behave this way?

The irony is that many of the people making the comments to coaches would wilt, cry, complain, throw a tantrum, or react in some other similar fashion if they were to be criticized in this way. They couldn't handle it. But coaches are supposed to just stand there and do their thing and "take it" and not say a word. And you know what? For the most part, they do just that.

It takes a lot of patience and discipline to not turn around and say, "Why don't you shut up, you stupid idiot?" But we hold back because we understand the concept of sportsmanship and the importance of modeling it to our players. Don't get me wrong. We have coaches who display poor sportsmanship. I dealt with them in an earlier chapter. But amazingly enough, most coaches handle this type of situation with a lot more class and dignity than the person who yelled it. And that is what we expect of our coaches.

It's sad in some ways. If a coach were to respond to the idiot fan, the coach would be criticized more and by more people because he "lost his cool" or he didn't stay focused on his team. The parent in the crowd yelling at the coach is considered acceptable, but the coach yelling at the parent is not. This double standard is just plain wrong.

Participants

The final group of people that often have to deal with poor sportsmanship on the part of parents are the athletes themselves. This, to me, is as sad as it gets. What is your problem that you, as an adult, feel that you have to yell or make comments at kids? I would say you need counseling yourself, and you don't need to be in that gym or stadium. These kids are merely playing a game. Some of them do it better than others; some of them do it cleaner than others. Coaches and officials will handle the play. It is not your place to yell things at players, whether they are your own kid, their teammates or their opponents. Yelling out brief words of encouragement, support, or elation is perfectly fine, but yelling or simply saying things that are hurtful, derogatory, or inflammatory is completely out of line.

Let me give you a couple of examples. In a basketball game, after a player misses a shot that does not hit the rim, the classic chant is, "Airball. Airball." We have seen this for years at college and pro games, and it is now in high-school games. It crosses the line of good sportsmanship even when students yell this out; however, it stampedes across the line of good sportsmanship when adults/parents yell this out. Or how about the parent who yells a sarcastic, "Nice shot, 42," when player #42 bricks one off the side of the backboard. Again, this is player bashing and totally uncalled for.

Here's one that goes into downright sickness. A few years ago, we had a parent at the school I was at who was freakishly obsessed with her hatred for our rival school. Every game with this school was a life-or-death thing for many of these fans, but for this person more so than any other. Both schools always competed very well against each other in most sports. This parent would constantly talk about how poor the sportsmanship was at the other school. Everyone associated with the other school was a target for her wrath. During one basketball game, one of the opposing team's players fell hard to the floor and was grabbing at his leg. Other parents reported her as saying in a loud voice, "I hope you broke your leg!" There is absolutely no place for a comment like that.

We also see parents point their poor behavior towards teammates of their own children. All too often we hear parents say things about how another kid shouldn't shoot the ball, or how bad that last play was, or some other derogatory comment directed toward another player. There is no good that can come of this. Sometimes the player hears it, which can be devastating. Sometimes the other player's parent hears it. Now you have a fight in the stands just waiting to happen. Sometimes the other players hear it. Now they are trying to figure out how to handle it. Sometimes the child of the parent who makes the comment hears it. How does she react? Maybe she agrees? Maybe she is embarrassed? Maybe she wonders how the rest of the team feels. No matter what, none of it is good.

Parents need to be more considerate about the entire situation as they sit in the stands and watch a game. They need to think about what their purpose there is. As a parent, you are not a player, coach, or official; you are a fan. But as a parent/fan, you also have an added responsibility. You are a fan who is there to encourage and support your child and his or her team. PERIOD.

That is a very large responsibility and one that you must take very seriously. You certainly are there to have fun. But your fun is the joy of watching your kid do something she loves to do. You are there to enjoy the fact that she has decided to do something that brings her joy, and you get to watch her do just that. Sometimes it is a nerve-wracking, gut-wrenching experience, but nonetheless, it is her thing, not yours. So be there for your child. And remember your role—to support and encourage your kid and her team in a positive manner. As for your role as the parent of an athlete the rest of the time, check out the next chapter.

25 ❖ How to Be the Parent of an Athlete

A whole chapter on being the parent of an athlete off the field? You bet. With all the problems we see with parents in athletics today, it is a topic unto itself. There are numerous elements that go into being the parent of an athlete if you want to do it right. If you want to help your child have a great experience in sports, you will need to do a few things and take on a few responsibilities.

Create a Strong Family

Let's start right off with the biggie—probably the toughest one of the bunch—but after all, a strong family should be the ultimate goal of all parents. Parents want to create a family that has love and respect for each member. They want a family that gets along with each other, as well as others. They want a family that has purpose and is willing to work to achieve desired outcomes. They want a family that other people look to as healthy, not dysfunctional.

But let's get one thing straight: the term "dysfunctional family" has become a kind of buzzword of the new millennium. Well, I would say that all families are somewhat dysfunctional in one way or another. Show me a perfect family and I'll show you a sitcom from the 1950's. (Can you say *Leave It to Beaver*?) Every family deals with a dynamic that makes them have their own quirks and idiosyncrasies.

So if "dysfunctional" is not what we want, then what do we want in a home and family that supports athletes? Well, the opposite of dysfunctional would be functional. While I am not a psychologist and I don't believe "functional" is a professional, clinical term, a functional family would be one that "works" and, for the most part, gets along. The members of the family respect each other. Sure, they argue and fight and have their problems, but they still love one another. A functional family realizes that the strength of the family is the bond they have. They spend time together and do things that they enjoy together. They make time for each other. They all pitch in to help the family function well, whether it is chores or homework, or simply listening to one another. They work to make sure that the family structure is intact.

The key to it is in the last sentence—they work. Great families don't just happen; it takes time and concerted effort, which starts with the parents. It is they who must set the tone early as to how this family is going to function. And then, more than anyone else in the family, they must work at it.

A strong family is a huge step toward a kid having a positive athletic experience. When there is a good structure at home, the kid feels comfort and security. This is important, because when things aren't going well at school or in sports, the kid feels that s/he has somewhere to go to get help or at least have someone listen. A strong family will help an athlete because the family will support the child through the ups and downs of his or her athletic experience.

Don't Force It

I strongly believe in the importance of kids playing in sports. It's a great way to teach them about all kinds of things that they may not pick up in class or even at home. The sporting arena is where one learns about discipline, hard work, sacrificing for others, winning and losing, overcoming obstacles, working as a team, and being a person of character, just to name a few. I think all kids should be involved in sports at some point in their lives. I know what sports did for me, and I've seen what they have done for thousands of kids. I also know what sports have done for my own son and what they could do for him if he continues to play. However, notice I said if he continues to play. I am as strong a proponent of athletics for young people as anyone you will ever meet, but I would never force my son to play a sport.

I will continue to encourage, tantalize, incentivize, and maybe even push a little bit if needed, but I have never and will never force my son to play a sport if he doesn't want to. The only exception is if he goes out for a team and stays with it for more than a couple of weeks, I will not let him quit—unless he is in a dangerous or damaging situation. I will talk with him about making a commitment to something and then sticking it out. If, after the season, he decides not to play the game again, that's fine. But once he joins a team and has been on the team for a while, his team is counting on him. If he quits, he will be letting the team down, and that is unacceptable in team sports.

However, if my son tells me he just doesn't want to go out for a certain sport, I will honor that. I will talk to him about it and ask him why he doesn't want to play, especially if it is a sport he has enjoyed in the past. I may try to talk him into it, but if his conviction is strong, I will respect it.

One thing I will explain to him, though, is that if the rest of the team is doing off-season work of some kind and he is not there, it would be unfair to them if he decides, when the season comes along, he now wants to play again. While I know that happens and may happen with him, I would explain to him that I will not talk to his coach on his behalf if he is not playing as much as he would like. He let his team and his coach down in the off-season when so much of the work is done to become the best one can be. If the coach chooses not to play him much or to put him on a lower-level team, that will be the coach's decision, and I will not interfere.

Of course, I am referring to a boy in the high-school ages. When children are younger, they should try all of the sports they can and should be encouraged to do so, but again, they should not be forced. If they choose not to play a certain sport at a younger age but then decide to play later, that's okay. The grade-school and middle-school years are when kids are finding out about so many new and different things. But even at these early ages, if they choose to join a team and stay on for several weeks, they should finish out the season.

Parents, it is so important that you help encourage your kids to get involved in various activities. If my son didn't want to play sports, but he wanted to play music, or act in plays, or do whatever, that's fine. As long as he is doing something constructive and healthy, I'm fine with it. Of course, as a coach, I love that he plays sports. I like the health benefits of sports, as well as the qualities I mentioned that sports will help to instill. Also, it is a bond or connection that he and I have, but if he decides in the future that he doesn't want to play, it will not be the end of my world. After all, it's his life, not mine. Besides, he may introduce me to something that I never would have known about and that would be a good thing, too.

NOTE: I first wrote the paragraphs above about my son when he was still in middle school. He just finished his senior year of sports. I never had to have any of those discussions about quitting with him, for he stayed in his sports (basketball and soccer) throughout his middle-school and high-school years. In fact, he enjoyed his experience so much that he is going to play both sports in college, too. I feel blessed that my son was able to derive so much joy from his athletic experiences that he wants to continue them both at the next level.

Release Your Child to the Game

There may be no more important part of being a parent of an athlete than releasing him or her to the game. I first heard this statement from Bruce Brown, the director of Proactive Coaching. But what does it mean? It means that when kids who play sports are younger, up to around age 8 or 9, parents are a huge part of their games. But as they get older, it is time for the parent to "let go." It is not your game with them anymore, unless you are their coach. If you are also the coach, you are there for many kids, not just your own, so now your role has changed. Remember that you can only be one thing at a time—when you are the coach, you are not the parent.

But most people are simply the parent. Releasing your kid to the game means that you are saying to your kid that you understand it is his or her thing, not yours. You will support him or her in playing this game. You will be there in whatever way s/he asks you to be there. But you will not overstep your role or your boundaries. You will buy the shoes, drive them to practice, cheer at games, and listen to them when they want to talk after the game, not when you want to talk. It means basically that you realize that you will stay out of the way.

Here's an example of releasing your kid to the game. A father I know (we'll call him Randy) is also a very good coach. He has three kids, all of whom played sports in high school. When his middle child was a senior, Randy heard Bruce Brown speak at a pre-season parent meeting about releasing your child to the game. When Randy heard it, a light bulb got turned on. As a coach for all the years he has coached, he has struggled with the fact that so many parents tried to be over-involved in their kids' athletic lives. Ironically, he hadn't realized that he, too, had done this, to a lesser degree, with his own kids. As an excellent coach himself, Randy knew that it would be inappropriate to go complain to a coach about something right after a game. However, when it came to his own kids, he was always right there standing outside the locker room ready to talk to them about what they did and didn't do well.

As Bruce was giving examples of parents not releasing their kid to the game, he heard some that really hit home. So many parents are right there after a game telling their kids what they did wrong and what they should have done. Bruce spoke about how many kids he surveyed through the years that said the thing they hate most about sports is the ride home with mom and dad. For so many of these kids, they receive a post-game analysis the whole way home. If they don't ride home with mom and dad, dad is sitting there waiting to talk when they get home, or worse yet, when they walk out of the locker room.

Randy realized this was him. He would meet his kid after he came out of the locker room and slowly work his way into what his son should have done different. Part of this was due to the fact that Randy was divorced, so he didn't get the same "home time" that other parents get with their kids. He figured that he would get his "coaching" in right after the game, so his son would be able to benefit from all of his knowledge while the game was fresh in both of their minds.

But Bruce spoke about the concept that every kid is different when it comes to the time and space they need after a game. Some kids want to talk right after the game, some need a few hours, and some need a few days. Unfortunately for some parents, some kids don't ever want to talk about the game with them. As tough as that is, again parents need to remember, it is the kid's game, not the parents'.

Randy realized that he needed to give his son time and space. After the first game of the year, as his son walked off the court into the locker room, Randy gave him a wave to say good-bye, and he left the gym. His new wife was incredulous. "What are you doing?" she asked. "How can you not stay and talk to him?"

Randy responded that his son will call him to talk when he's ready. If he doesn't call, so be it. He will be okay. The next morning his son called and wanted to talk about the game. Randy offered him his ideas, but only based on what his son asked. He didn't go overboard and give him too many of his own ideas. This was a big step for Randy, and we're talking about a guy who has had to deal with this problem with his own players and their parents for over twenty years. Randy called me later that day, and said, "You would have been proud of me. I released my kid to the game last night." He went on to explain how it went and how good it felt. He continued doing this with his son for the rest of the year and then for the next two years with his youngest daughter. He was still always there for them as a supportive parent, but he wasn't overbearing in his support.

How Not to Do It

Now let's look at a couple of parents who haven't released their kids to the game. There are numerous examples I could give, but I am going to focus on two—a girl's dad and a boy's dad. They're both in middle school, and hopefully when they get to high school, this will stop. Middle school is kind of a transitional time from being a little kid to being a teenager, so I will allow that some parents have trouble letting go. However, this is the time when it needs to happen.

The sports involved in these scenarios are softball and baseball. The girl is a 7th grader who is a B-team player. She is playing middle-school sports for the first time. After any inning in which she had to make a play, her dad goes over to the dugout, she steps out of the dugout door, and he tells her something about what happened. The same thing goes on with every at bat. Dad has not released her to the game. Now think about this from her coach's perspective. Her coach works with her at practice for two hours a day for two weeks before the game season begins and then every day that they don't have games. He has coached softball for years, and he knows the game. There is no reason for this parent to be talking to his daughter during the game, other than to say, "Nice job, Mary" or "That's okay, Jane. You'll get it next time." But this parent feels it is his right or prerogative to do so.

On the other side of the diamond, we have a boy whose dad does similar things. His reasoning is that the boy is a special-education student, and he needs a lot of extra help and guidance. While I sympathize with his learning disability, at some time, he needs to learn to be coached by his coaches alone and middle school is that time. More importantly, Dad needs to cut the strings and release him to the game. When the boy gets to high school, if Dad goes out on the football field, basketball court, and baseball field and pulls his son aside to show him things, his coaches and the athletic director will have to address the situation and put an end to it.

Both of these parents are prime examples of something that every school in the nation deals with—parents who haven't released their children to the game. Athletic directors around the country have done informal surveys of athletes at their schools, asking them what they liked and didn't like about various elements of their athletic experience. Time and time again, kids speak about how much they hate it when their parents get too involved in their sports. They talk about their embarrassment at how their parents act in the stands and about how they hate it when their parents complain to the coach. More than anything else, they talk about their dislike for their parents' post-game analysis.

One interesting side note to Bruce Brown's survey mentioned above is how many kids speak about how much they like when their grandparents come and watch them. When asked why, they explain that their grandparents usually keep quiet at the games and just cheer when good things happen. After the game, when the grandparents come up to talk to the kids, whether they win or lose, the thing the kids hear most often is something along the lines of, "Good game, dear. We love watching you play." What a great thing to say to your kid after a game—"I love watching you play." What kid wouldn't want to hear that?

I have tried that myself with kids. I began doing this with my stepdaughter and other relatives and friends of the family who I have watched play. Because I am a coach, I think that sometimes they are waiting for me to offer some coaching points; however, I just say that it was fun watching them, or that they have a nice team, or they play well together, or the opponent was really tough, or something like that. I don't offer anything that could be construed as coaching unless they ask for it and only if I feel comfortable enough with the sport to offer any. Even then, I keep it to one short thing and leave it at that. This kid is getting enough coaching from other people that s/he doesn't need another one telling him or her what to do.

I also do this with my son, and I will admit it has not always been easy. I have spent so much time coaching him and helping him that I want to offer ideas right away after games. However, I force myself to tell him things like, "Nice job," and "Did you have fun?" and "I really enjoyed watching you play." Then, later, when the time seems right, I may ask him if he wants to talk about some things to help him out the next time. I walk a fine line here because I was his coach through 8th grade, and in many ways, he still considers me his coach. I have to be careful as to whether or not I am wearing the coach hat or the parent hat, so that I speak accordingly.

I mentioned earlier the idea of me being comfortable enough with the sport to offer advice. It's amazing to me that so many parents who are offering their kids post-game commentary are doing so about sports that they know very little about. I know a little bit about quite a few sports, but my specialty is basketball. I feel confident that I could help most kids in any basketball situation if they had a question for me. I have also coached football and soccer at the high-school level for enough years that I could probably help kids in those sports a bit, but I would probably be stretching it if I tried to go too far. I have had my experiences playing baseball, tennis, and golf, so I might be able to offer some rudimentary advice on those sports.

Overall, I have been a coach for over thirty years, so I certainly could offer comments about teamwork, discipline, work ethic, sportsmanship, hustle, and so forth. Actually, most of the time those are the only kinds of things I will comment on anyway, if asked to do so, because I believe those are the most important elements of the games kids play. But I don't have any volleyball, wrestling, hockey, swimming, gymnastics, or track-and-field experience, so who am I to tell a kid what specifically he or she should be doing in those sports? And I'm a coach and former athletic director! What about the parent who has never coached a day in his or her life? Who is s/he to be telling kids how to perform their games? (I don't know if I want my wife to read those last two questions or not!)

Well, all a parent sees is his or her baby out there. All parents want to see their kids succeed, so they often will do what they can to help their kids achieve. So they feel a comment here or a demonstration there will help. Pretty soon, the comment becomes a lecture on what the kid is doing wrong and what s/he should be doing better. The demonstration becomes a twenty-minute coaching clinic on how to execute the perfect lay-up, single-leg takedown, or throw to second base. As you are straining muscles to show your kid how s/he should have done something that s/he was trying his or her hardest to do for the last hour-and-a-half, stop doing that right now and remember these words—RELEASE YOUR CHILD TO THE GAME!

Support All Involved

The best athletic parents are supportive of not only their children but also their children's teammates, coaches, game workers, administrators, and anyone else who has a hand in their children's athletic education. Good athletic parents understand that involvement in sports is one part of the overall educational experience of their child, not the only part, or even the most important one. These parents recognize that their children are learning all kinds of things by their involvement in athletics and therefore will support all the people who are playing such a large role in this extremely emotional, exciting, and important aspect of their children's lives.

Volunteer

Another important part of being a good athletic parent is to volunteer or offer to help out in some way. Whether it be volunteering to help coach the team, or offering to drive kids to games, or cooking a pre-game meal, or some other way, volunteering helps to bring parents closer to the kids, the coaches, and the other parents. It gives them a chance to see some of the action from up close. It's much easier to understand why a coach, a player, or team does things the way they do when one is more involved than if the only contact they have with the team is sitting in the stands watching a contest for two hours. Volunteering also shows the team that you support them. While not all coaches want volunteers, and some would find it hard to have certain parents so close to the action, there are a variety of ways for parents to volunteer, so please find a way to volunteer your time to help your child's team. You and the team will be glad you did.

Talk to the Coach

One simple way to be a good athletic parent is to talk to the coach. By talking to the coach though, I am referring to general conversation, not necessarily athletic issue-related discussions. Of course if parents have concerns, they should talk with the coach in a meeting, but if they have established a conversational relationship with the coach already, it is a lot easier for them and the coach to discuss the concerns that the parents have.

Imagine in a work setting an employee who never talks with another employee. Now the other employee is doing something that is bothering the first employee. It will be difficult to address the co-worker because no communication or relationship has been established. However, if the two workers converse on a somewhat regular basis, it will be far easier to approach the fellow employee about the issue. The same holds true with the parent/coach relationship. If a parent has had conversations with the coach at other times, it will be a far less tense or awkward discussion.

Before, During & After Games

Game day or night brings a whole different level of anxiety into the athletic realm for all of the parties involved. It is the culmination of the efforts of the practices in the days leading up to it. It is helpful for parents to recognize that there are a few things that they can do to help their child, along with the coach and the team, to have a positive game experience. Bruce Brown has come up with the following excellent list of tips to help parents handle themselves and their kids around games:

Before—Know their goals, roles and needs, and accept them. Release them to the game, their coach and their teammates.

During—Model poise, confidence, and correct behavior. Focus on our team.

After—Give them all the time and space they need. Be a confidence builder.

The Library versus the Arena

As I discussed in Chapter 21, the typical problematic athletic parent today is the one who will do anything and spare no expense to get his kid a college scholarship. Fortunately, most parents aren't like this, but the number of them has grown at an alarming rate. It's easy to see why. With the proliferation of ESPN and all of its spin-offs and competitors, sports talk radio, different sports publications, scouting agencies, and the Internet, we have become inundated with college and professional sports in ways we never imagined just twenty years ago. As a result, parents have all too often become obsessed with the notion that Junior can be the next Michael Jordan or Tom Brady. Even if they don't think that big, the belief is out there that, given the right circumstances, Junior can at least get to college by being a great athlete.

The truth of the matter is that Junior stands a far better chance of getting to college by using his brains than by using his muscles. In Chapter 21, I mentioned how Scholarshipstats.com talked about how difficult the odds are of a high-school athlete playing a college sport, let alone receiving scholarship to do so. An example of some of those statistics can be found at the NCAA's "Estimated Probability of Competing in College Athletics" report from April of 2018. I also gave a couple of statistics about the difficulties for boys and girls trying to play college basketball. Once again, for a complete listing for all of the sports in both genders go to the link at www.ncaa.org/about/resources/research/estimated-probability-competing-college-athletics.

In her article, "7 Things You Need to Know About Sports Scholarships," Lynn O'Schaugnessy states, "There's so much disinformation about athletics scholarships circulating in this country." She researched the situation and found that, "There are roughly 138,000 athletic scholarships available for Division I and Division II sports. That might sound like a lot, but it isn't. For instance, more than one million boys play high-school football, but there are only about 19,500 football scholarships [1.9%]. Nearly 603,000 girls compete in track and field in high school, but they're competing for around 4,500 scholarships [less than 1%]."

O'Shaugnessy goes on to point out that the money involved is not always all that much. "The average athletic scholarship is about $10,400. Only four sports offer full rides to all athletes who receive scholarships: football, men's and women's basketball, and women's volleyball. If you exclude football and men's basketball, the average scholarship drops to around $8,700."

O'Shaugnessy's research and subsequent article came out in 2010. Since then, when you consider all NCAA and NAIA levels, the average athletic scholarship dollar amount has actually gone down. In 2017, the average men's scholarship was $6,283, and the average women's scholarship was $7,541. For more specifics, check out "Average Athletic Scholarship per College Athlete" at the following link:

www.scholarshipstats.com/average-per-athlete.html.

Interestingly enough, O'Shaughnessy points out that the best place to receive maximum bang for your scholarship buck comes at the Division III level:

> The best way for many athletes to win a scholarship is to apply to colleges that don't award athletic scholarships. Yes, that's right. Division III schools, which are typically smaller private colleges, routinely give merit awards for academics and other student accomplishments. The average merit grant that private colleges are awarding routinely slashes the tuition tab by more than 50 percent. Here's the bottom line: Students and parents … should be realistic about a child's scholarship chances. For most athletes, academic scholarships from the colleges themselves are going to represent the preferable way to shrink the cost of college. (O'Shaugnessy, "7 Things You Need to Know About Sports Scholarships").

These statistics help to show that if parents are truly most interested in their kids getting into college, they are far better off sending them to the library for three hours than to the gym. Having said that, I believe that oftentimes when some parents say that they would just like to see their kid get a chance to go to college, what they really mean is that they would like to see their kid go to college on a sports scholarship because it sounds so much cooler to say, "My son got a full ride to play quarterback at USC," than to say, "My kid got a full ride in chemistry to MIT."

Of course, most parents would be thrilled that their kids got into college, let alone got additional money to go to college. But I would remind parents that it's your kid's life, not yours. Let them choose the path that they want. Then, give them every opportunity to make it happen. If that happens to be in the athletic realm, then that's great, but you need to help them understand that the road through the arena is much harder and much less certain than the one that goes through the library. Oh, and the athletic-scholarship road still goes through the library, because if he doesn't get good grades in high school, he's not going to be playing in college anyway.

Be a Model Fan

I spoke earlier of some of the problem-parents when it comes to how they act in the stands at games. One of the best ways to be good athletic parents is to be model fans. Being model fans means always being supportive, first and foremost, of the parents' own children. They don't yell embarrassing, hurtful comments at their own kids. Model fans are also supportive of the team and the coaches. They yell encouraging comments to all of the players, not just their own kids. Model fans never yell derogatory or disparaging remarks at officials, coaches, or players. They recognize that good sportsmanship is not for players and coaches alone but for the fans as well. In fact, model fans realize that they need to do just what the name implies—they need to "model" proper behavior.

Imagine what a game would be like for the kids if their parents would all be model fans. They would play without fear of embarrassment at how their parents acted in the stands. They would know that, no matter what happened or how they played, their parents would still be supportive of them, their teammates, and their coaches. And they would not worry about their parents' post-game analysis. While it is probably never going to happen that all parents become model fans, it is still important to encourage parents to do everything they can to help their children's and their team's performance in the games they play.

Conclusion to Parents' Section

Well, that wraps up the section on Parents. While it wasn't as long as the section on Coaches, many of the issues in it are just as important, if not more important, than the issues for coaches. I hope that any of you parents out there will take to heart the things that I have talked about in here, just like I hope the coaches took to heart what I said to them. If we all work together on these types of things, we can all help our kids to have the best athletic experience possible.

That is maybe the most important point I could make in this book. All too often, coaches and parents have relationships that could be viewed as adversarial. They struggle to see eye-to-eye and to get along with regards to how they view the experience for their players/kids. Ironically, they both want the same thing—a great experience for their kids. They just often have a different idea of what that is. If both groups can begin to see things from the other group's perspective, it can go a long way towards doing just that—providing kids the opportunity to have the best possible athletic experience.

4th Quarter ~ Others Affecting Kids' Sports

While coaches, athletes, and parents all play the most important and impactful roles in the good, bad, and ugly in kids' sports, there are certainly other factors that affect the experience that our kids are having when playing their sports. While these are not as impactful as the people who are actually involved in the sports and the kids' lives, each of these factors can be shown to have some impact on how our kids play their sports or view how their sports experience should go. Because of that, it is important for us to point out these different elements, so that we can address them and then work to improve them or eliminate them altogether. That way, the negative impact that they may be having on our kids' sports can be diminished.

26 ❖ Administration & Other Teachers

When looking at the problems associated with youth and high-school sports, we should also look at the role that administrators and teachers play. You may be thinking, "What? How do teachers or administrators play a role in the problems with school-age sports?" Well, quite honestly, they don't cause anywhere near the amount of problems that the other groups discussed here do. They are minor players in the problems of youth sports, but nevertheless, there are a few issues to consider.

Lack of Support

Administrators and teachers who don't support the athletic programs undercut those programs, whether directly or indirectly. What are some of the ways they don't support the athletic programs? Some of them don't go to games, or they don't ask kids how their games or competitions went, or they ignore athletics in some other way.

While this lack of support may not undermine the programs all that much, sometimes it is a bit more direct or purposeful. Some teachers think athletics are a waste of time. They believe that kids should be at school to "get an education, not play games." They don't realize that athletics provide kids many aspects of an education that they don't get from the classroom, books, or computers. While it is common for a school's star athletes to get idolized, some of these teachers think that athletes get special treatment. They believe that because a kid can hit, throw, kick, or run better than other kids, those kids are receiving special favors.

What they often don't see are the sacrifices these athletes make, or that the athletes are actually being held to a higher standard than non-athletes. At most schools, athletes have to maintain certain grade-point standards in order to play. These standards are higher than the standards that non-athletes are held to. If it weren't for athletics, many of these kids wouldn't do their schoolwork or wouldn't do it as well.

Finally, some types of teachers struggle to connect with athletes. Some athletes can have intimidating or loud personalities, transferring their tendencies to be overly aggressive and confident into the classroom. These types of behaviors can make some teachers nervous and can disrupt their classes. While this may be due to a teacher's classroom-management inadequacy, it still creates situations where teachers struggle with athletes. Teachers need to build positive relationships with all of their students, including the athletes. Athletes and non-athletes alike need to be dealt with according to the school and classroom rules. If the athletes don't behave properly, the teacher needs to correct the inappropriate behavior.

The difference between the athletes and the non-athletes who exhibit poor classroom behavior is the athletes have a carrot that can be taken away that the non-athletes don't have. Good teachers and administrators use this concept to help manage and motivate, rather than to punish and intimidate. It is important for teachers to establish good relationships with their students and then use the proper methods of discipline accordingly.

Understanding the Importance of Athletics

As I alluded to earlier, some teachers and administrators don't see the role that athletics play in a kid's life. For many kids, athletics is the one thing that makes them want to go to school. It is the reason they get to school on time, pay attention in class, do their homework, and try to pass their classes. While that is not the way we want it to be, it is just a fact. Unfortunately, some teachers and administrators struggle with this concept. "They should be here for school first and athletics second," they say.

Well, sorry, but it just ain't that way for all kids, and for some kids, it will never be that way. Now, rather than bang your head against a wall and get all fired up about it, how about accepting that and then playing that for all it's worth? My gosh, you have a kid who is in your class for fifty minutes who is actually paying attention to you. Who cares why he is paying attention to you? Just focus on inspiring him and then filling up his knowledge cup with all that you can. This has always been one of my favorite things in teaching—having kids in class who aren't really all that into school, but who know they need to do well, and then turning them on to learning and seeing the proverbial light bulb go on for them throughout the school year.

Athletics is not the enemy, people—it's actually the ally. I can't tell you how many non-coach teachers I have known in the four different schools and three different states in which I have taught who have said to me at some point, "I don't know what you do to Johnny, but keep it up. He is really working hard. Last week, I told him I was going to talk to you if he didn't turn things around, and he has been a totally different kid." Well, I didn't really have to do all that much to Johnny, other than tell him he won't play if he has an F in any class or if I hear he is screwing around and being a problem for the teacher. By his coach making academics and classroom behavior a priority and then holding him accountable for his actions, Johnny does what he has to do. Oh, to be sure, it doesn't always work this way, and there will still be some Johnnies and Jennys who don't get it, but for the most part, it works.

Unfortunately, some teachers will take this ally relationship a bit too far. I have had my fair share of teachers come up to me and say, "One of your basketball players has been acting up in class lately. It's Johnny. Why don't you make him do some extra wind sprints at practice this week?" Or I've heard, "Sally flunked a quiz this week. I don't think she should play in the game tomorrow." Now, as I said before, I am all for athletics and academics being allies. But I struggle with a teacher telling me these sorts of things. If we have a rule or standard in place about certain situations and a kid violates that rule, by all means, we will deal with it, but I struggle with a teacher asking me to handle his or her classroom problems.

What I have usually done in that situation is say to the teacher that I will take care of it, and then I will go talk to the player. I will say something like, "Mrs. Jones says that you have been screwing around in class too much. This is a poor reflection on me, the team, and on our entire program. I better not hear anything like this again, or I will deal with it in a more severe way. Is that clear?" Usually, that is all it took for the kid to change his or her behavior.

However, here is what I always wanted to do, but never could bring myself to do it. Sometime I would love to go up to one of those teachers who asked me to handle their discipline and say, "You know one of your science students was just dogging it in practice last night. It was Timmy. He just wouldn't work hard or pay attention when I was teaching a new move. Why don't you give him some extra science problems to do after class today?" Would that be any different than what those teachers were doing with me?

Athletics provide kids with another avenue for learning all kinds of things to help prepare them for life, like accountability for one's actions, the value of working hard, commitment to a shared goal, helping others succeed, dealing with loss, handling praise, being disciplined, competing fearlessly, and respecting leadership. I could list many more. So it's important for teachers and administrators to remember that while the classroom is a great place for kids to learn, it is not the only place where learning occurs.

Get Them Involved

One way to help non-coach teachers and administrators get on board with athletics is to get them involved early on in their time at the school. The best way, of course, is to hire them as coaches. If you have openings, try to encourage teaching applicants to also coach. If they have no athletic experience or interest, how about having them get involved in band, drama, or a club? If they will at least get involved in some extracurricular activity, then supporting athletics will be a much easier step. By being involved with kids on a whole different level than just the classroom, they will start to get to know their students and other students in a different way. They will also develop a better understanding of what the coaches and athletes go through.

If a teacher candidate has athletic experience, it may be a great fit to hire him or her as a coach, as well. But what about candidates without much athletic experience who show an interest in coaching? Should you hire them to coach? That all depends upon the situation, but for the most part, I would say "Yes." Consider the fact that you have people here who are interested in coaching. All too often, that is the first hurdle to clear when trying to hire qualified coaches. Sometimes we just can't get enough applicants to begin with, so when you have someone interested, that is the first big step. Also, these are people who have either just learned through schooling or through prior teaching experience how to deal with kids. They will be dealing with kids every single day for about six hours. They know about planning, leading, discipline, management skills, and motivation. If they don't know those things, why were they hired to teach?

I would say who is better qualified to coach than a teacher? The obvious response is, "Someone who has played or coached the game before." Certainly, if you can find someone with coaching experience, that is a plus. But just because someone knows the game or played the game doesn't necessarily mean s/he can coach. Coaching is much more about the skill sets of planning, leading, discipline, management, and motivation than it is about offenses and defenses. While sport-specific knowledge is important for coaches to possess, all the sport knowledge in the world doesn't matter if you can't get kids to show up, work hard, be disciplined, play together, and behave properly. So when considering teachers who have no coaching experience, don't just automatically rule them out. Many of the good coaches I have known in my career had no prior experience in the sport they coached.

Teach Them the Game

As an Athletic Director, when I dealt with administrators and teachers who were not very supportive of athletics, I found great value in teaching them as much as I could about the sports our students played.

How about inviting the staff out for the first games of each of the fall sports? Make it a "we" thing. Throw a staff tailgate party or have a pre-game dinner at the school cafeteria or the principal's house. Have knowledgeable people about the sport explain some of the rules and nuances of the game to everyone. How about the night before the game, order pizza and salads and have the coach come in and talk about the game, show portions of game films, and explain a bit about what to watch for in the game? You could also have a "Teacher of the Night" award (or something else you would want to call it) that the players vote on for each game. Then, invite that teacher to that upcoming game, introduce her/him before the game, and present her/him with a "Teacher of the Night" certificate and a gift card to a local restaurant.

The point is, there are a variety of ways to get teachers and administrators involved and supportive and to get them out to games. Once there, maybe an assistant coach or staff member who knows the sport is designated as the person who will explain what he sees. The more the teachers feel connected to the games, the more supportive they will be, and the better overall climate the school will find between the staff and the athletic programs. A positive overall school climate should be a goal for any school and its staff.

Obviously, teachers and administrators play a huge role in the success of a school. The success of a school comprises much more than just test scores and graduation rates. Extra-curricular activities are a big part of the life-blood of any school. Athletics is usually the biggest extracurricular activity in most schools. Teachers and administrators who recognize and support athletics in the school help to contribute to the overall positive atmosphere of the school. The more involved they are in the extracurricular aspects of their students' lives, the better experience they and their students will have. So, if you are a teacher or administrator who is not involved in the athletic realm, please do your part and help support the athletic programs. You and your school will be glad you did.

27 ❖ The Upper Levels of Sports

College Sports

As a coach or athletic director for most of the last 30+ years, I have loved watching college sports to help me learn more about coaching. The college game has had a certain purity that the pro game has lacked, while still having incredibly gifted athletes. However, that purity has diminished through the years. When it comes to the big-time sports that have professional leagues, the college game has become more and more like the pro game, from styles of play, to poor displays of "me-first" attitudes and bad sportsmanship, to scandals outside the arena of play. College sports are big business now, and unfortunately, much of the seedy side of big business has crept in as well.

It used to be that I would tell kids to watch the college games instead of the pro games to learn how to play the game. The college teams played more of a team game than the pros did. There was more of a "we" element than a "me" element, but that seems to be changing. From multi-million-dollar coaching contracts, to players leaving college early (sometimes as "one-and-done" players) for the big money and stardom of the professional ranks, college sports is not what it used to be. Too much emphasis on flash and style, individual athleticism, and winning "the big one," have all hurt college sports, even though they may have helped TV ratings and exposure. As a coach, I feel these trends have led our kids to focus less on the team and on the work it takes to succeed.

The other problem with college sports is the number of people who feel they are good enough to receive an athletic scholarship because they watch college sports all the time on TV. They see the excitement of the games, the individual accolades, the fun of the "College Game Day" atmosphere, and think, "I want to be a part of that."

There is nothing wrong with wanting that and having the desire to play a college sport. The problem is the number of young people and their parents who think they are good enough to play in college is absurd. For those who work incredibly hard all year long and who have a high level of talent, it is fine to believe this way. But the majority of young athletes don't fall into this category. Most of them don't have the ability and work ethic necessary to play at the next level—and as shown by the statistics that I pointed out in the earlier chapters, relatively very few high-school athletes make it into college play.

Not having the necessary skills isn't nearly as big a problem as the fact that so many of them think they do. They have an extremely warped perspective of their own abilities and of the abilities of college athletes. Kids with marginal high school talent think, "I could play there," when looking at most levels of college sports. While most kids with average high-school abilities don't foresee themselves at the big-time Division I programs, unfortunately, many still misjudge how good the athletes are at the other levels of college sports, and they believe they are every bit as good as those athletes. Again, that's not to say that many of them aren't good enough to play at some level of college. It's just that most high-school players aren't anywhere near good enough or committed enough to play at most levels of college sports.

Professional Sports

To my way of thinking, professional sports are a far bigger problem than college sports. Professional sports are far more popular with kids than college sports. Kids' biggest heroes play at the professional levels. Unfortunately, these heroes aren't always very heroic. The behaviors displayed by too many of our professional athletes are appalling. As my son was growing up, I grew to a point where I didn't want him to watch a lot of our professional athletes play. What a shame.

When I was a kid, these were the players I wanted to watch, the ones I looked up to and wanted to be like. These athletes had reached the pinnacle of their profession, and represented the standard for others to shoot for. However, the standards have dropped so far that many of our high-school and college players and coaches have become the leaders of how to behave and play. In most professions, we want to look to the people at the top for examples of how to be the best. That's not necessarily the case anymore with regards to sports.

Celebrating

Let's just look at a few of the recent happenings in professional sports to see how bad it has become. In football, the last few years have seen the rise of the end-zone celebrations to unprecedented and downright foolish levels. There is nothing wrong with expressing your joy and exuberance at getting into the end zone. However, it is obvious that this joy is now more about putting the spotlight on the individual who got there.

These celebrations are pre-planned, choreographed shows designed to bring more attention to the player, usually a receiver. Never mind that it took a quarterback to throw it to him, a line to block for the quarterback, and a coach to design the play. "Forget about them. I'm THE MAN!" Some of these players have become better known for their stupid antics and big mouths more than for their abilities to play the game of football. It's also that these are the players our young people end up focusing on as the "heroes" of the game.

Ironically, when I started writing this book, these celebrations were just like I described. However, in the last couple of years, the NFL changed its mind on celebrations and started allowing certain levels and types of celebrations. They have been more enjoyable and more team-oriented than the "look-at-me" celebrations of the past, and that is a good thing. We want there to be joy in sports. But we need to make sure that the joy of one player or team is not ridiculing or humiliating the team's players or the other team in general.

Law-Breaking and Fighting

Another area where we have seen more problems with the higher levels of sports is in troubles with the law. Over the last couple of decades, there have been more arrests of professional sports players for more crimes than ever before. From domestic violence to shootings to dogfighting and killing, the list of athletes in trouble with the law is massive. So many of the professional players have grown up in less-than-solid home settings and then are thrust into stardom and riches that they don't have a foundation on which to stand or a way to stay grounded. Coaches aren't immune to poor behavior, either. As I started researching the ideas I wanted to put into this book, the New England Patriots were in the middle of a magical, history-making season, but it had been tainted with stories of cheating, running up the score against weak opponents, spying on opponents at practice, and illegally deflating footballs to give their quarterback an advantage.

In basketball, there have been brawls through the years, none more infamous than the one between the Detroit Pistons and Indiana Pacers in 2004. This was professional sports at its ugliest, with players going into the crowd to fight fans and fans throwing things and coming out onto the court to hit players. Two years later, we saw another brawl in Madison Square Garden involving the New York Knicks and the Denver Nuggets, including one of the league's young superstars, Carmelo Anthony. While this one stayed between the players, it showed that the league certainly still continued having its problems with players not able to handle their emotions and being poor leaders and role models for young people.

I loved the NBA as a kid, but now I am so disappointed in the *it's all about me* game it has become. Ironically, the player I most admired growing up in the 1970s was Julius Erving, better known as Dr. J. He was one of the greatest showmen ever to play the game, with a style that had previously been kept to the playgrounds and the ABA (American Basketball Association) where Dr. J first played professionally. But Dr. J's style never included the in-your-face finger-pointing, chest thumping, look-at-me element that has since become so popular. His contemporaries, Magic Johnson, Larry Bird, and Michael Jordan, all were incredible talents and played with similar style, grace, and humility, while still being intensely competitive. We need players like them again to become the mantle for the league.

Performance-Enhancing Drugs

Major league baseball isn't what it once was, either. The last few years of the 20th century saw a resurgence in America's love of the national pastime. Two events marked the biggest contributors to this interest: Cal Ripken's chase for Lou Gehrig's Ironman record and Mark McGwire and Sammy Sosa's home-run battle. Unfortunately, while Ripken's story of hard work and determination was a great feel-good at the time, it lost out in our memories and the collective conscience of the nation as McGwire's and Sosa's battle and McGwire's subsequent season-home-run record were tainted by allegations of steroid abuse by both players. In the years after their record-setting year, they lost face with their "non-testimony" in front of a grand jury investigating steroids in baseball.

Then, along came Barry Bonds to save the day by crushing McGwire's new record. But the excitement over that record was short-lived as Bonds, too, was part of the steroid talk. Soon, Bonds was not only part of the talk, he was the poster boy for it, as he zeroed in on Hank Aaron's career-home-run record in 2007. A month after the season in which he set the new record, Barry Bonds was indicted by a federal grand jury for lying about his steroid use. While the record home-run ball is in the Major League Baseball Hall of Fame (albeit, with an asterisk on it), Bonds himself is not. He has fallen short of the needed votes each year he has been eligible. In 2019, he received 59.1% of the votes. He needs to get 75% of the votes to make it in, and he only has three more chances to do it. It's hard to believe that the all-time home-runs leader in major league baseball history might not end up in the Hall of Fame.

This situation illustrates how our professional sports heroes all too often are no longer heroic. They have capitalized on their talents and said, "I don't have to play by the rules. I have been treated as a god my whole life, and it's about time I show people that I am a god. If I want to abuse the game that made me famous and allowed me all the riches I now have, so what? I'm bigger than the game. I'm certainly bigger than all the little people that showed me how to play the game and how to act when I was younger." What a shame that so often these are our leaders that our young people are taking their cues from as to how to be an athlete.

28 ❖ Society in General

Another contributor to the problems we have in youth sports today is what I would call "societal influences," which would be things like role models for kids, the money in sports, media exposure, societal norms and mores, and just the general nature of how our society operates today as opposed to "how things used to be."

While I often point to problems with our youth sports stemming from what kids are seeing at the pro and college levels, I think it is a mistake not to look at the youth sports themselves first before examining the upper levels. Youth sports and school sports contribute to their own problems because of many of the elements we have already discussed. Poor coaching, improper focus, misbehaving parents, skewed assessment of kids' abilities, and unrealistic expectations all contribute to the problems we see at these younger levels.

We must help kids at the youth and high school levels have a better experience by helping them grapple with many of these issues. Addressing the problem at its heart is the key, but we also need to start understanding some of the elements that contribute to the problem that are a little more distant from the youth sports themselves.

Little Eyes Are Watching You

I often tell our high-school and middle-school athletes to watch how they behave because "little eyes are watching you." I ask kids to behave responsibly and with character because other people are constantly judging them and our teams, our programs, our school and our community based on their behaviors. Most importantly, little children are watching them to see what it means to be an athlete and how to act like one. Well, I say to you professional and college athletes, those high-school and middle-school eyes are taking their cues from you as to what it means to be an athlete, and they are passing it on to the younger kids with their behaviors. Obviously, the little ones are watching you, too. It's time for you to live up to your responsibilities. If you are going to be the pinnacle of your profession, you need to act like it.

It's a shame when I have high-school freshmen and sophomores ask me why a pro player acts in some disgraceful way and then say, "Shouldn't they know better?" So many of our good young players now realize that these infamous athletes are not acting the way an athlete should. Unfortunately, many kids still look at their physical and statistical success and feel that the way to behave as an athlete is the way these poor role models behave.

We need to continue to work on educating our kids about the character elements necessary to be one's best. However, we also need to continue to educate our college and professional athletes on this as well. We also need to continue to work with coaches on proper behaviors as well, not only for them to work on instilling in their players, but also for the coaches themselves. Coaches are not above reproach, no matter at what level they coach.

The list of coaches who are behaving as poorly as the players continues to grow every year. If coaches are going to be the leaders and models for their programs and for athletics in general, they must behave in a way that embodies character, integrity, and good judgment. Just like the players are role models, so are the coaches. So, I say to coaches and players alike, please work to be the best leaders and role models that you can be. The young people (and their parents) are counting on it.

Money in Sports

One element of sports that may be overlooked as contributing to the problems is the incredible amount of money that is now commonplace at the upper levels of the games we play. Multi-million-dollar salaries for players and coaches, exorbitant prices paid for teams by owners, and the outrageous spending of their fortunes that we see from professional athletes are all contributing to the problem of kids and their parents wanting a piece of the pie. The money involved in big sports is ruining the games people play. While it is certainly a case of "what the market will bear," it is tearing away at the fabric of athletics as we have known it through the years. The trickle-down effect that we see in so many areas of our sports world is at play when it comes to money. It used to be that the big money was at the pro and NCAA Division I levels of major sports. Now it is also trickling into other levels and sports.

I have no problem with paying coaches better, because they do an important, time-consuming, and stressful job. However, we are seeing some amazing dollars being thrown around all levels of sports in so many ways. We hear stories of high-school football coaches in Texas being paid $75,000 a year just to coach! $30,000,000 high-school stadiums being built is becoming commonplace in various places around the country. Youth travel teams paying to play in tournaments all around the country is happening at an alarming rate. A few years ago, even when we were in the worst recession since the Great Depression, we had people throwing this kind of money around for youth and school sports. I would say it is time to get a handle on this, but I wonder how that is going to happen.

Unfortunately, as with many of the problems I see in youth sports, school sports, and our society in general, when it comes to money issues, I'm afraid things are only going to get worse before they get better. Ironically, I'm the first one to say that we need to find a way to fund many of the youth sports and better fund many of our school sports. I advocate for that, not to line certain individuals' pockets, but to pay for proper education of coaches, parents and kids, and better character coaching to have a positive impact on kids, and safe equipment and facilities for kids to be able to practice and play their games.

Right now, we are perpetually on shoestring budgets for our youth and school sports. We need to find ways to change that. Sports teams and programs at the professional levels and big-time college levels need to take some of their profits and filter them down to youth and school sports throughout the country. This would be a way to ensure that the games they administer continue to grow, develop, and improve, while at the same time, helping young people have better athletic experiences. By giving back to where it all starts, they will build up their own teams and programs.

Media Exposure

Another problem societally is the media exposure that we now see with regards to sports. In the last twenty-five years, sports on television, radio, and the Internet has exploded! ESPN, Fox, NBC, and CBS seem to have more TV and radio stations and affiliates than can be counted with a calculator. Sports-talk-radio shows and stations are at an all-time high. YouTube is filled with every move, interview, and sneeze that any player of any sport ever made. Recruiting websites for high school athletes to showcase their skills to colleges are popping up faster than beer cans at a NASCAR race.

While this exposure can be a positive, it has led to a warped idea on the importance of sports in our society. Don't get me wrong. I am right up there with the leaders of the movement to make sure that youth and school sports stay prevalent in kids' lives because of all the positives that they can provide. However, the focus on sports has become warped to a dangerous level. It's not that people shouldn't embrace sports and get excited and passionate about them. It's just that so many people have gone overboard with a level of insanity about their sports that is downright scary.

One of the scarier things I see about this oversaturation of sports in America, is that now we have high-school sports games being broadcast on ESPN. ESPN, "The Worldwide Leader in Sports," has done so many wonderful things for bringing the excitement of sports into our lives. They have brought fan interest in sports to an unprecedented level. However, they have also been a huge part of the problem. With 24/7 coverage, 365 days a year, on more channels than you find on a trout steam, ESPN has helped feed the monster that has become sports. But the addition of high-school games, skills combine events, and recruiting stories has gone too far, in my opinion.

With my life's experience as a high-school coach and athletic director, you might think I would like all the attention that high-school sports is receiving. While attention can be nice, this kind of attention is not. These are kids aged 14 to 18 playing games on national television! We already have a problem with some kids' overinflated egos and a sense of entitlement due to the fact that they can throw, jump, run, kick, or perform some other skill. Putting them on television is just going to add to the disease. It is also going to create more competition from other high schools, high-school coaches, and high-school administrators to get that same level of attention (and money) that playing on ESPN is creating.

As an athletic director and coach, I had enough headaches to deal with without having to have some parent or parents believing that we weren't doing enough at our school for our kids, because we weren't playing on ESPN. My other concern is this—what's next? Middle School? Grade School? Youth Rec Leagues? Oh wait a minute, I forgot. We already have those on TV. Every fall, ESPN broadcasts the Little League World Series for a couple of weeks. Well, maybe for a world series, but do we need it for regular season high-school games? I think not.

Sportsmanship in Society

While I have discussed the importance of instilling and reinforcing good sportsmanship for players, coaches, and fans, this section is about the concept of sportsmanship in general, or rather the concept that society has lost its focus on sportsmanship recently. Somewhere along the way, we went from a society that said that competition is good if it is done fairly, cleanly, and humbly to a society that says, "I'm gonna' kick your butt, and then I'm gonna' rub your face in it and tell everyone in the world about it." What happened to playing with class, dignity and respect for the game and for all involved in the game? What happened to fans cheering for their team in a positive manner instead of constantly taunting opponents, and criticizing and yelling at officials?

While so much of our society has become too concerned about being politically correct in many different areas, it has gone just the opposite when it comes to sportsmanship. There is very little that is "correct" in any way any more, when it comes to the way our society handles sportsmanship. I really don't know how we are going to change it either, other than for it to start at a grassroots level with our schools and our youth leagues. Many of us who are in leadership roles in these organizations try to do what we can to instill good sportsmanship. That's a start, but somehow, we have to move it on up the ladder to the colleges and pros, too.

As I wrote that last sentence, I couldn't help but think, "Isn't that a shame? Isn't that an amazing statement in and of itself about the state of sportsmanship today?" In just about every other realm of sports, we at the high school and youth levels take our cues from the pros and colleges. Players watch pro and college players and try to play like them. Coaches go to clinics, read books, and watch DVDs of pro and college coaches to try to glean anything they can to make themselves better and their programs more successful. Administrators follow the leads of game administration at the upper levels to try to create an inviting, exciting atmosphere in their schools and at their games.

But here I am talking about US having to show THEM how to behave properly when it comes to sportsmanship. Shouldn't it be the other way around? I know there are some college coaches and administrators who work very hard to do all they can to create the proper level of sportsmanship in their programs. I applaud them for all they do. But I also ask them to help us all by getting out and championing this cause.

If the absolute best teams at the absolute top levels were to stand up and say, "This is how one behaves and acts at this level," and then publicly chastised those who didn't, it might help start to swing the pendulum back the way it needs to go. When the best of the best lead by this kind of example, we will be taking the kind of steps necessary to bring sports back to their original purpose and intent—a bunch of kids running around having fun in front of their friends, families, and others, who are all cheering them on for their efforts and their successes.

Fans can help, too. For those of you who misbehave in the ways described above, just stop it. There is no logical argument that you can make that validates and justifies your lewd, malicious, or dis-respectful behavior. For those of you who don't act this way, thank you! We (athletic administrators and coaches) really do appreciate you. If you are sitting with someone who is acting up in this manner, consider addressing him or her in some way.

Guilt is sometimes a good motivator. Humor helps, too. If they don't get the point, you may have to say something a little more seri-ous. If you're not comfortable saying something to the offender, ask someone else to do so, or call over a game administrator and ask him or her to talk to the person. Game officials and administrators don't hear everything that fans say, so they can't address it if they don't hear it, or if you don't make them aware of it. If they are made aware of it, hopefully they will have the courage to deal with it.

The Final Buzzer

Youth and school sports are an extremely important part of our society. In many ways and for many people, they have become too important, and their overblown importance has led to a lot of the issues presented here. But I still believe in the positive power of sports for kids. The joy, emotions, and lessons sports provide for people are far too important and impactful for us to not have an opportunity to provide them for our kids. We must work to keep providing these opportunities.

However, we must also get a better handle on how we are doing so. From the kids to the coaches to the parents to the fans, we all play a role in the experience we are providing for our kids. It is imperative that we all come together in a meaningful way to figure out exactly what that means and how to do it. It is not enough anymore to say, "Well, that's just the way it is and the way it has become. There's nothing I can do about it." Hogwash! We can all do something about it and make it a commitment.

We can start by providing education and training for all coaches at all levels of youth and school sports. This type of training needs to start when coaches are just beginning their coaching, which is often at the start of their own child's sports experience. While this would require an investment of money and time on the part of our youth sport leagues and our schools, we must find ways to do it. Programs on sport education could be developed to create funding and trainings, possibly by professional leagues or by governmental agencies. Whenever we have an epidemic of any other type, programs to mitigate the problem are developed and implemented. It is time for that to happen with youth and school sports, for we are at an epidemic stage with regards to the problems with youth sports. We can start by training our coaches properly, and then I believe we'll see positive changes in our kids' athletics.

This type of organization can also provide mandatory education for parents on their role and function in their kids' sports. Make it a pre-requisite for parents to attend a few hours of training on proper parent and fan involvement and behavior before, during, and after games. For instance, many schools around the country bring in speakers from organizations like Proactive Coaching to speak to parents at their pre-season athletic meetings. "The Role of Parents in Athletics" is one of Proactive Coaching's most viewed and most popular presentations. It speaks directly to parents about what they need to do to help their kid have a great athletic experience.

However, hearing presentations like that after your child is already in high school may be too late. Just like we need to get this type of education going for coaches at the beginning of their children's sport experience, we need parents to start hearing these messages and receiving training on their role in the sport experience from the start of their children playing organized sports. Then, we need to keep providing ongoing education to keep those ideas at the forefront of their minds. Like anything, to assume that since someone has heard something once, it is therefore fully ingrained for life is ridiculous. There is a reason why kids go to school for at least 12 years and why teams repeat certain skills and strategies many times throughout a season. We need to constantly reinforce these messages of what the proper youth sport experience looks like.

While there are other groups who also need work to create a better youth sport experience (non-parent fans, administrators, officials, and the kids themselves), coaches and parents are the most important, most impactful, and most often the biggest problems and the biggest solutions in the whole experience. Let's start with them first. Then we can spread the net wider in order to create an even better experience.

When we start treating youth and school sports like an educational system in our country (which it most certainly is) and start funding it and training for it in the same way that we do for our academic educational system, we will begin to see the positive growth and change that we all seek to create for it.

Nobody wants youth and school sports to be a bad experience for their kids or for themselves. Everyone is seeking a positive, productive, fun, and educational experience from sports. Yet, every week we hear new stories of situations where just the opposite has happened, at all levels of sports. It is time for us to change that narrative, to take back youth and school sports, and to create the kind of experience that we all want our kids to have. It is time for action. Let's start to create that change today!

Post-Game Analysis

I first started jotting down the ideas for this book almost twenty years ago and started writing it a couple years later. A lot has changed since then for me personally, professionally, and in the world of sports. A few years before I began writing the book, I had just gone through a divorce. A couple years later, I re-married, gaining a stepdaughter, and then having a son of my own. Throughout the writing of the book, I have had to go back and change his age as I would do rewrites.

He is now 18 years old. Much of what I write about has been altered a bit by my personal feelings about my own son growing up in the world of youth sports. My ideas haven't changed, but they have become so much more personal and up-close because of him. I have seen some of the horror stories in youth and school sports first-hand both as a coach and as a parent watching my son play or watching his friends and their families go through such things. I know our little corner of the world is not unique, which is scary to me to think that the lunacy that I have witnessed personally is nothing strange to the entire world of youth sports.

Professionally, I went through a lot of changes while writing this book. Suffice it to say that I have been through a lot both in and out of the teaching and coaching worlds over the course of twenty years. While there is a lot I wish would have happened differently, I am glad I had all those experiences from which to draw upon as I wrote this, as I tried to provide kids a positive athletic experience. While I'm not going to say, "I wouldn't trade those experiences for the world," I will say that I would definitely be glad to trade some of them! I will say that each has shaped the coach, athletic director, parent, writer and speaker that I have been and that I am today. So for that, I am grateful for all of the experiences that led to this book.

In the world of athletics in general, we have seen our share of changes, as well. While there have been some positive changes, unfortunately, we have seen too many negative ones. But many of the positive changes we have seen have been in reaction to negatives that have crept into our athletic world. For example, while the rules we have seen instituted about trash-talking, taunting, end-zone celebrating, and the like, have been good, the only reason we have those rules is because of how out-of-hand these issues have become. The headlines that we have seen in the newspapers and on *SportsCenter* on a regular basis have not been very positive: "Little League Pitcher Throws at Teammate on Coach's Advice," and "Basketball Team Wins 100–0," and "Dad Beats Hockey Coach to Death."

What has happened to our world of sport? Well, it has gotten out of control. I began this book as a way to help people recognize the problems that we have been creating for ourselves in the world of school sports. But I also wrote it as a way for people to arm themselves with positive weapons to stop the problems from happening and to work at fixing the problems that already exist. Only time will tell if we have been successful at doing so.

However, one thing is certain. If we don't start to do something collectively as a youth/school sports society and as a society in general, things are going to continue to get worse before they get better. My hope is that everyone who reads this will help us in the fight to save our sports for our kids now and in the future. That would be my biggest goal in writing this book. I thank you for reading this and for helping to do your part to make our youth and school sports the positive experience they should be for all of our kids.

Appendix A
Sample Policy Sheet

Park High Rangers Basketball
Policy Sheet
2010–2011

Park High Rangers Basketball
Core Covenants ~ 2010–2011

When people watch us, whether it be at practice, playing in games, or anywhere else we are together, what will they see? What are the elements that we will be known for? When you make a commitment to something or to others, it must be binding. It must be strong. The strongest commitments of all are covenants. Covenants are agreements that people who are committed to one another make to state that they will do all it takes to achieve their common goals.

I believe that the following Core Covenants are what everyone in our basketball program must commit to in order to achieve the success we are seeking. You will be expected to live these covenants every day. When you make the decision to be part of this program, it requires your strongest bond—it requires your covenant. Once the team has been selected, we will look at these covenants and determine if we want to amend them for our specific purposes for this season. To begin our journey together into this season, these are the Core Covenants for the Park High Rangers Basketball Program. *Live Them!*

Sportsmanship—I will act in such a way that I will always show poise, control, and grace, no matter the situation or the outcome. I will applaud my teammates, coaches, opponents, and officials for jobs well-done, and I won't criticize, taunt, or belittle those same people.

Discipline—I will do what needs to be done, and I will do it everyday, the right way, and every time it needs to be done. I will have a focused attention and focused effort.

Strong Work Habits—I will put forth nothing but my best effort each moment that I am involved with this team. There is no place for coasting or taking a play off.

Commitment to Team—I recognize that individual goals

and accomplishments are secondary and usually by-products of team success. I will be selfless and unselfish. I will not let my teammates down.

Positive Attitude—While I am in complete control of all of these core covenants, this one is what controls all of the others. I must be a positive contributor to my team and the entire program, as well as a positive ambassador of our program as a whole.

Goals:

1. Get better every day—*Win the Day!*

2. Work as hard as we possibly can in both practice and games.

3. Compete fearlessly!

4. Play with poise, control, and grace as an unselfish, cohesive unit.

5. Be tenacious defenders, and take pride in our defense.

6. Qualify for State Tournament.

(Continued on next page.)

Park High Varsity Basketball Lettering Criteria

25 points needed to letter:

¼ point for each varsity quarter played

½ point for winning the game

1 point for participating in another sport (last spring, this fall)

3 points for any summer camp attended or summer traveling squad participation

5 points for no unexcused or late practices

2 points deducted for each unexcused practice

1 point for no team-rule violations

4 points for 4.0 GPA, 3 points for 3.0 GPA

3 points for all gear returned in acceptable condition within one week of last game. 3 points deducted for each day anything is late

0-5 points for attitude, coachability, etc.

3 Points for making State Tournament

*Extenuating circumstances will be taken into consideration when determining if someone is deserving of a letter who may or may not have otherwise received one.

WHAT YOU CAN EXPECT FROM YOUR COACH

1. He will be prepared.

2. He will be positive-demanding.

3. He will be fair and willing to listen to you in the proper place and time if you do not think he is being fair.

4. He will be honest with you.

5. He will expect punctuality for all activities.

6. He will use practice performance as the primary criteria for determining playing time.

7. He will see a lack of effort in practice performance and/or practice intensity as an indication that you are not in the proper frame of mind to compete.

8. He will be quick to criticize constructively. He will be quicker to praise.

9. He will expect a high level of academic performance, and he will expect proper classroom behavior.

10. He will be ready and willing to help you with problems that you may encounter that are not directly related to basketball. If it appears your attitude or level of play is slipping, he will address it with you.

11. He will be willing to help you prepare for life after high school, whether that includes basketball or not. However, his focus is on this season with this team first and foremost, as should be yours.

12. He will respect your need to be involved in activities other than basketball and your need to lead a well-balanced student life. However, he will also expect that when you are at a basketball related activity, you are committed to basketball 100%.

13. He will attempt to make strategy and personnel decisions in the best interests of all involved in the Park High Basketball program, not just one or a few.

14. He will coach to put the team into a position to win every game. However, he will not sacrifice integrity, discipline, and sportsmanship in order to win a game.

15. He will expect nothing more from you than an effort, intensity level, and attitude that indicate that you are enthusiastically involved and working to improve within the team framework.

WHAT IS EXPECTED OF YOU AS A PLAYER

1. Proper behavior and respect towards others should help overcome any temptation to act in a manner that brings embarrassment to the group.

2. You must understand that the primary reason you are in school is academic work. Your classroom behavior must be exemplary.

3. You must understand that practice is the most important part of the season.

4. Effective practice requires the concentration of the whole team at all times. Players who attempt to slide by in practice and turn it on for games are usually unsuccessful.

5. You represent Park High Basketball, Park High School, and the Livingston community in all you do. You are no longer just yourself. You are part of something much bigger. Everything you think, say, and do will be judged by others and will reflect on us individually and on the group as a whole. Be judicious in your words and actions.

6. You must understand that individual accomplishments and any subsequent recognition are the results of hard work by everyone and by great teamwork.

7. You will accept and respect the decisions of your coach to be in the best interests of the team and Park High Basketball in general. If you do not, please bring your concerns to your coach in private. Do not voice or display your displeasure in a manner that could be seen as a negative attitude.

8. You need to develop a respect for all internally involved within the program. These are the only people who really understand what happens with us on a day-to-day basis, and they are a good support group. It would be foolish or unwise to think that we will all be good friends or that differences in personality or philosophy will not develop. The important thing is that in the basketball context we pursue our common goals as a unit and put aside our differences. We may not all be the best of friends, but we can develop enough mutual and collective respect to overcome any internal adversity that develops.

9. Under no circumstances should you see it as your right or responsibility to criticize or make light of a teammate's best effort. What your teammates want and need from you is your support and encouragement.

10. You are on this team to play basketball, not coach it. Let your coach do his job, and he will let you do yours.

WHAT IS EXPECTED OF YOU AS A PARENT

1. Be supportive of your son's effort and performance. What he needs most from you are words of encouragement instead of words of criticism, especially during and after games. However, your son also needs to be pushed to do his best, not coddled and praised when he has done nothing deserving praise. He needs to learn to "deserve victory," and you can be a big help in teaching him that.

2. Be supportive of your son's teammates. This is critical to team success, for if you are critical of his teammates, he may lose trust

in his teammates, or he may also feel it is his right to be critical of his teammates as well. All that would get us is dissension and finger-pointing. If you say anything about his teammates, please make it something positive.

3. Be supportive of your son's coach. This can be a very difficult thing for some parents to do. Playing team sports brings out many emotions in families. If you do not think that your son is playing enough or the team isn't winning enough or something else isn't happening the way you think it should be, it is very easy to fall into criticizing the coach. While we as coaches can and do take our share of criticism, we ask that you come talk with us first, so that we may be able to explain ourselves. That way there can be an understanding as to why things are being done as they are. Then, any criticism you may have will be from a standpoint of knowledge and insight instead of from hearsay and confusion. If you do decide to talk with us, please do not do so before or after a game. Call to schedule an appointment.

4. Cheer in a positive manner at games. Your son and his teammates need to hear positive, encouraging comments about their play. There is no place in high school athletics for yelling negative, insulting remarks at players, coaches, and referees. That's right, referees. Remember that referees are human beings too, and they will make mistakes in a game. So will your son and your son's coach. We all do.

5. Familiarize yourself with the rules of the game. This can help you understand why officials make the calls they make and coaches and players do some of the things they do.

6. Understand that winning is one of many of our goals here, not the only one. We want to focus on improvement, team play, discipline, hard work, and being good sports and positive ambassadors of our school and community as our biggest goals.

7. When you do have a concern or a problem that you want to discuss, after your son has talked to your coach, if you still have

an issue, you can talk with your son's coach to work towards an understanding and a solution. This should be done in private and not before or after a game. Ultimately, this is the only way to move forward positively.

8. Release your son to the game. It is his game; let him have it as his own. It is amazing how much more our children enjoy their athletic experience when we help them understand that it truly is theirs. You will also be amazed at how much more YOU will enjoy it. If you want your son to take steps forward, it is important for you to step back.

(Continued on next page.)

Rules and Policies

Familiarize yourself with the rules and regulations the High School Association has established regarding your participation. All Park High School & Livingston School District and activities department guidelines and sanctions will be enforced.

One major rule to live by: "Don't let your teammates down."

This is a great guide for all athletes to help them keep in mind how they need to behave as a member of a team. What doesn't it cover? Behavior, practice habits, game situations, drugs, alcohol, and academics are all covered by this one statement. So let this be your guide. However, I believe that it is helpful for student-athletes to be aware of certain specifics with regards to their own team. Therefore, I have outlined a few specifics for you, so you are aware of them beforehand. As you will see though, they fall under the one major rule of not letting your teammates down.

Practices

Without effective practice instruction, we will not improve as we must. Every minute of practice is planned and organized. To help ensure that our practices are effective, the following guidelines will apply:

A. You must be dressed in appropriate practice gear. We will have practice jerseys and practice shorts. No shirts or shorts from other schools will be permitted.

B. Unless excused by your coach, you are to be at every practice and be there on time. You will be excused if you have a valid reason. If something comes up, call your coach at school or at home. Coach Rosberg—223-XXXX; Coach Willyerd—224-XXXX. Missing practice will translate into less playing time in games.

C. *Any player who misses a practice without a valid excuse will be suspended for one game. Any player who misses a second practice without a valid excuse will be suspended for two games. Any player who misses a third practice without a valid excuse will be dismissed from the team. The coach will be the one who determines whether or not the excuse is valid. Consistently missing practices or being late to practice will result in limited playing time and possible suspension. You need to practice in order to play.

The rule above is one that I have altered since the original. I have now made it more open-ended by not delineating any specific punishments for specific infractions.

D. Being late to practice without a valid excuse will result in reduced playing time in games. Detentions are not valid excuses for being late to practice, unless your coach has okayed this.

E. Never leave the practice floor unless excused by your coach. Never take a ball out of the gym when you go.

F. If you are unsure of a drill or play, ask a question. When asking a question, make sure it is done in an appropriate manner. On the floor, "How" questions are acceptable; "Why" questions usually are not.

G. Do not talk to people outside of the basketball program while you are at practice. This includes friends and family. Once you are in the gym, your team deserves your time. Tell your family and friends this, so they can help you by not coming in to talk to you.

H. Each day at practice, recommit to your Core Covenants.

Games

Games are the icing on the cake. They are the reason you play. They are also the time that we are most in the public eye, and they are the most emotional times we spend together. Therefore, keep in mind the following guidelines for game time:

A. Any player who misses a game without an excuse may be suspended for one game. Missing any more games without an excuse may result in being dismissed from the team.

B. A dress code will be in effect for all games, both home and away. If you are found in violation of the code, you will not play in that game.

C. When we play at home, if your team is the first to play, you must be to the gym right after school, unless your coach tells you otherwise. If you are in a later game, you must be at the gym at the start of the game prior to yours. Sit together in the stands, both at home and on the road. This is a time to be with teammates. When we play on the road, be ready to leave at the designated time. If you are not there, we will leave without you. You will not be allowed to show up at the opponent's school and play. Once the game prior to yours starts, do not eat food or drink pop. Nutritious snacks that your coach deems appropriate will be the exceptions to this rule.

D. Make sure your hair is cut in a neat and clean manner. No eccentric colors or styles will be permitted unless there is a cultural explanation for it.

E. Any player involved in stealing or maliciously damaging property will be dismissed from the team.

F. Never talk to or argue with game officials. Any player receiving a technical foul for inappropriate behavior will be immediately benched. Any player receiving another technical foul for inappropriate behavior at any time during the season will be benched for the remainder of that game and suspended for the next one. A third inappropriate behavior technical foul will result in dismissal from the team.

G. Never acknowledge or talk with spectators at games. This includes family and friends. Please ask your family and friends not to try to communicate with you during games.

H. For games wear plain white socks that reach no higher than below the calf. Acceptable shoe colors and styles for games will be determined prior to the season.

I. Treat opponents and opposing coaches and bench personnel with dignity and respect.

J. Prior to each game, re-commit to your Core Covenants.

General

These rules and guidelines are designed to be both fair and consistent, and they will be applied across the board. During the course of the season, these rules may be violated and go undetected or unpunished. Sometimes the players will know about it, but the coaching staff won't. Something similar happens in all family situations. We do not want it to be this way, but that is the way it is. If you are in violation of a rule, do not expect it to go unpunished because others have violated it and were not caught, or it was not dealt with in the past. Be responsible for your own actions. True team leaders will step up and address their teammates and sometimes their coaches when necessary in these situations.

All sanctions and punishments are completely at the coach's discretion.

Declaration with Regards to the Park High Basketball Policy Sheet

I have read the Park High School Basketball Policy Sheet. I understand its contents, and I agree to abide by the expectations and the rules and regulations outlined in it. Furthermore, I understand I may face certain consequences for not following these rules and regulations.

I have also read the Park High School Activities Participation Code. I agree to abide by the rules outlined in those as well, with the understanding that if I don't I will suffer specific consequences. Please sign on the line below, tear off this sheet, and return it to your coach.

_____

Player Signature

_____

Parent Signature

Bibliography

Atkinson, Jay. "How parents are ruining youth sports: Adults should remember what athletics are really about." www.bostonglobe.com/magazine/ 2014/05/03/ how-parents-are-ruining-youth-sports/ vbRln8qYXkrrNFJcsuvNyM/story.html

"Average Athletic Scholarship per College Athlete," www.scholarshipstats .com/average-per-athlete.html

Bertin, Randy. "A Funeral for Sportsmanship." Athletic Search, 2006. www.athleticsearch.com/bertrinon113.htm

Brown, Bruce. *Teaching Character Through Sport*. Monterrey, CA: Coaches' Choice, 2003.

Brown, Bruce. *1001 Motivational Messages & Quotes*. Monterrey, CA: Coaches' Choice, 2001.

"Chances of a High School Athlete Playing College Sports." www.scholarshipstats.com/varsityodds.html

Kilmeade, Brian. *The Games Do Count*. New York: Harper Collins, 2004.

Krzyzewski, Mike. *Leading with the Heart,* New York: Warner Business Books, 2000.

Manoloff, Dennis. "Noted surgeon Dr. James Andrews wants your young athlete to stay healthy by playing less." *The Plain Dealer,* February 27, 2013.

Martens, Rainer. *Successful Coaching.* Champaign, IL: Human Kinetics, 1981.

Bibliography

O'Shaugnessy, Lynn. "7 Things You Need to Know
    About Sports Scholarships," June 22, 2010
    www.usnews.com/education/blogs/the-college-
    solution/2010/06/22/7-things-you-need-to-know-about-
    sports-scholarships

O'Sullivan, John. *Changing The Game*.
    Morgan James Publishing, 2014.

"Parents: Missing in Action!" The Real Truth website.
    rcg.org/realtruth/articles/266-pmia.html,
    February 28, 2014.

Pitino, Rick. *Success is a Choice*. New York: Broadway Books, 1997.

Relin, David Oliver. "Who's Killing Kids' Sports?"
    Parade, August 7, 2005, 4.

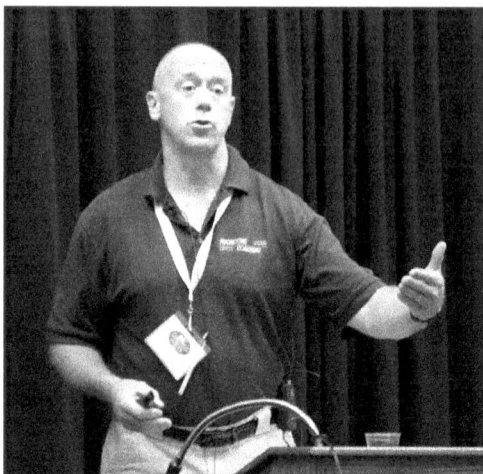

About the Author

Scott Rosberg has served in the roles of teacher, coach, and athletic director for over 35 years. In addition to *Time Out!*, Scott has published multiple books on character-based coaching and athletics, all of which can be found on his website www.greatresourcesforcoaches.com. He has also published two books of inspirational messages and quotes—one for senior athletes and one for graduates. Scott has published numerous articles, blogs, and videos on character-based coaching and athletics. He does workshops, classes, and presentations at schools, conferences, and businesses. Check out the Great Resources for Coaches Facebook page at www.facebook.com/greatresourcesforcoaches.

Scott is also a member of the Proactive Coaching team of speakers. Proactive Coaching is dedicated to helping organizations create character-based team cultures, while providing a blueprint for team leadership by helping develop confident, tough-minded, fearless competitors and train coaches and leaders for excellence and significance. Proactive Coaching can be found on the web at www.proactivecoaching.info and on the Proactive Coaching Facebook page at www.facebook.com/proactivecoach.

Other Books by Scott Rosberg

The Responsibilities of Coaching

A Head Coach's Guide for Working with Assistants

The Assistant Coach's Guide to Coaching

Playing Time:
A Guide for Coaches, Athletes, & Parents

Establishing Your Coaching Philosophy

Team & Program Policies: Elements to Consider

The Sportsmanship Dilemma: Guidelines
for Coaches/Athletes/Parents

Building Your Coaching Staff Chemistry
Book & eBook

Senior Salute
Gift Booklet for Senior Athletes

Inspiration for the Graduate
Gift Book for Graduates

You can find each of these titles at
www.GreatResourcesForCoaches.com.

You can also join the Great Resources for Coaches
community to start receiving Scott's newsletter,
blog, and any new updated materials.

Email Scott at
scott@greatresourcesforcoaches.com
if you have any questions.

www.ingramcontent.com/pod-product-compliance
Lightning Source LLC
Chambersburg PA
CBHW052035090426
42739CB00010B/1920